C0-CEN-148

A Staff Development Guide

to Workshops for Technology

and Information Literacy:

Ready-to-Present!

Kay Bishop and Sue Janczak
State University of New York at Buffalo

With Editorial Assistance From
Jennifer Cahall

Linworth
PUBLISHING, INC

Your Trusted
Library-to-Classroom Connection.
Books, Magazines, and Online.

Dedication

To all our former students who have made our jobs as school media specialists and library school educators exciting, rewarding, and challenging.

Cataloging-in-Publication Data

Editor: Judi Repman

Published by Linworth Publishing, Inc.
480 East Wilson Bridge Road, Suite L
Worthington, Ohio 43085

Copyright © 2005 by Linworth Publishing, Inc.

All rights reserved. Purchasing this book entitles a librarian to reproduce activity sheets for use in the library within a school or entitles a teacher to reproduce activity sheets for single classroom use within a school. Other portions of the book (up to 15 pages) may be copied for staff development purposes within a single school. Standard citation information should appear on each page. The reproduction of any part of this book for an entire school or school system or for commercial use is strictly prohibited. No part of this book may be electronically reproduced, transmitted, or recorded without written permission from the publisher.

ISBN: 1-58683-156-9

5 4 3 2 1

Table of Contents

Acknowledgements

W e are indebted to the school media graduate students at both the University of Buffalo and the University of South Florida for providing us with ideas for this book, gathering resources, and piloting our workshops. We are especially grateful to David Mead for creating the original graphics for our workshops, to Stacy Brand for gathering resources, and to Penny Winklebleck for piloting some of the chapters.

About the Authors

K ay Bishop is the Director of the School Library Media Program at the University of Buffalo. She has authored or co-authored four books and numerous articles in professional journals. Prior to joining the faculty at the University at Buffalo, Kay was a faculty member at the University of South Florida, the University of Kentucky, the University of Southern Mississippi, and Murray State University. She has 20 years of experience as a school media specialist.

S ue Janczak is the Coordinator of the School Library Media Program at the University of Buffalo. She has over 20 years of experience as a school media specialist at all grade levels in New York State. Sue has served as an educational consultant and workshop presenter for technology integration for Bull Information Systems.

J ennifer Cahall lives in Fairport, New York where she works as an instructional designer, creating interactive educational and training products including Web sites, CD-ROMs, and classroom courses.

Introduction

A re you a media specialist who is constantly busy? Do you never seem to have time to develop the inservice workshops that you know would benefit the teachers in your school? If so, this book was written especially for you. As former school media specialists, we understand these challenges and have been in similar positions. Yet, we also acknowledge that major leadership and instructional roles of today's media specialists involve teaching information literacy skills to both students and teachers. Conducting staff development workshops on information literacy skills and emerging technologies can make it possible for you to collaborate with teachers to design lessons that will improve students' information literacy skills.

We are pleased to share with you this book and accompanying CD-ROM, which contain information, ideas, and materials for media specialists to conduct staff development workshops. The guidelines for conducting effective staff development presentations and the ready-made materials can save you enormous amounts of time. The inclusion of the CD-ROM, complete with the author-created materials for the various staff development topics, makes it possible for you to download the materials and adapt them for your particular school setting, with a minimum amount of effort. This is a unique feature of our book. All workshops have been piloted in educational settings and we incorporated improvements provided by workshop participants. All the workshops in the piloted settings were completed in our suggested time frames; however, additional time may be required if you add refreshments and time for socialization. Varying from the suggested number of participants for specific workshop topics may also alter workshop time allotments.

Chapter 1 of the book provides general background information on how to conduct effective staff development workshops. The remaining chapters follow the format and headings used in Chapter 1, but address specific workshop topics. Each chapter provides these sections:

- Background and information needs related to the topic
- Planning the workshop
- Conducting the workshop
- Evaluating the workshop

- Follow-up activities
- Final tips
- References and selected resources

Materials on the CD-ROM have varying designs, but each chapter includes the following items:

- A workshop announcement
- A workshop agenda
- A PowerPoint presentation
- A workshop evaluation form
- A handout of selected resources

Some chapter folders on the CD-ROM contain additional items specific to the chapter topic. Because of copyright limitations, original graphics have been used on all the staff development materials. Persons conducting nonprofit workshops can use these graphics or can easily download the materials from the CD-ROM and modify the items by inserting clipart, borders, or other graphics.

The following section provides samples of the type of items that can be found on the CD-ROM for each chapter. In this instance we have used some of the items from Chapter 3, "The Plagiarism Plague: Detection and Prevention."

Workshop Announcement Flyer or Invitation

Flyers enable you to advertise your workshop in a fun, informative way. Flyers can be printed for posting or copying, or they can even be e-mailed. Invitations, such as the two-fold invitation created for Chapter 3, are an alternative way to personally encourage teachers to participate in the workshop.

Plagiarism Plague!

Agenda

Refresments

PowerPoint Presentation and Activities

    ✓ Defining plagiarism

    ✓ Recognizing reasons why students plagiarize

    ✓ Indentifying means of deecting instances of plagiarism

        • Exploring "paper mills"
        • Paraphrasing

    ✓ Identifying ways to prevent plagiarism

    ✓ Identifying methods to teach students to avoid plagiarism

Evaluation

Workshop Agenda

The agenda provides your participants with a preview of workshop topics and activities. It also helps you stay focused and organized during the presentation. We suggest including the agenda in your workshop handout materials

Preventing Plagiarism

- Design assignments to utilize higher thinking skills.
- Provide alternative research products, rather than the traditional written paper or report.
- Require oral presentations
- Limit the age of references.
- Require process steps.
- Require an annotated bibliography.
- Let students know you are aware of methods for checking for plagiarism.

PowerPoint Presentation

The PowerPoint file offers a ready-made slide show for your workshop presentation. In each chapter the PowerPoint presentation can be found in a folder inside the chapter folder. We encourage you to print PowerPoint handouts for your participants to refer to during the presentation. There is ample room for taking notes if you use the "three slides per page" option when you print handouts. In the "Print What" box of the *Print* window, select "Handouts." Under "Handouts" in the "Slides per page" box, select 3. To save toner or ink you should print handouts in pure black and white. This can be done by selecting "Pure black and white" in the lower left corner of the *Print* window.

Paper Mills

- http://www.cheater.com/
- http://www.cyberspace.com/
- http://www.geniuspapers.com/
- http://www.cheathouse.com/
- http://www.schoolsucks.com/
- http://www.goldenessays.com/

Objective:

Identify means of detecting instances of plagiarism

Notes:

• Inform the participants that the Internet contains many sites where students can obtain term papers. Some of the sites provide free papers, while others charge a fee.

• Divide the participans into groups and assign each group to explore one or more of the paper mills listed above. The paper mill sites are also listed on the handout entitled "Online Help"

• Ask the participants for their reactions to the sites.

 The Plagiarism Plague!

Evaluation

1. Was the information in this workshop presented clearly?

2. Did the workshop successfully help you understand how to identify methods to teach students to avoid plagiarism?

3. Did the workshop help you understand ways to detect student plariarism?

4. How could the workshop be improved?

5. Would you like a follow-up workshop to explore anti-plagiarism software?

6. Would you like a follow-up workshop to further examine anti-plagiarism tutorials?

If you would be willing to serve on a committe to develp an academic honesty policy, please contact: (place the name of the appropriate contact person here)

If you would like to collaborate to design or redesign your lessons to avoid plagiarism, please contact me at: (place your e-mail address here)

PowerPoint Speaker Notes

A learning objective and speaker notes are provided for each slide in the PowerPoint presentation. This information helps you effectively prepare for the presentation in a time-efficient manner. It also offers guidance for interacting with the participants in meaningful ways throughout the workshop. You will want to print out speaker notes to be used in each of the workshop presentations. In the "Print What" box of the *Print* window, select "Notes Pages."

Workshop Evaluation

The evaluation is an important tool for you to understand the effectiveness of your workshop. Information learned from the evaluation can be used to improve future workshops. Evaluations can also help you determine what kinds of follow-up activities might be necessary to further enhance participant learning.

Selected Resources Handout

Resource handouts can be printed for each workshop participant. These handouts assist participants in further exploration of the workshop topic. They also encourage teachers to take their learning beyond the workshop and apply it in their classrooms.

The Plagiarism Plague: Detection and Prevention

SELECTED RESOURCES

Citations

The following are a few sites that provide examples of how to cite materials in several style formats.

Columbia University Press. (2002). *Basic CGOS style*. Retrieved June 11, 2003, from http://www.Columbia.edu/cu/cup/cgos/idx_basic.html

Ohio State University Libraries. (2003) *Citation and style guides*. Retrieved June 11, 2003, from http://www.lib.ohio-state.edurefweb.resources/style.htm

University of Arizona Library. (2002). *Citation Guide*. Retrieved June 11, 2003, from http://dizzy.library.arizona.edu/library/type1/tips/data/citation.html

Detection

These sites provide information about software programs or services to detect plagiarism in research papers.

Eve2 (n.d.) Retrieved June 11, 2003, from http://www.canexus.com/eve/indexs.html

RFE Integriguard (n.d.) Retrieved June 11, 2003, from http://rfe.org/Teaching/IntegriGuard.html

Glatt Plagiarism Services (n.d.). Retrieved June 11, 2003, from http://www.plagiarism.com/

Plagiarism.org (2003). Retrieved June 11, 2003, from http://www.plagiarism.org/index.html

Worksheet (2002). Retrieved June 11, 2003, from http://www.word.checksystems.com/

Educating Students

Purdue University Online Writing Lab. (2003). *Avoiding plagiarism*. Retrieved November 14, 2003, from http://owlenglish.purdue.edu/handouts/research/r_plagiar.html

University of Maine at Farmington Writing Center. (2003) *Synthesis: Using the work of others*. Retrieved November 14, 2003, from http://www.umfmaine.edu/~library/plagiarism/

 CD-ROM Directions

All materials on the CD-ROM use Microsoft Office applications. You will need to copy the materials to your computer in order to alter any of the information from the read-only CD-ROM. To use the CD-ROM follow these instructions:

1. Insert the CD-ROM into the appropriate drive on your computer.

2. **PC Users:** Double click on the My Computer icon. Double click on the CD-ROM drive icon.

   Macintosh Users: Double click on the new icon that appears on your desktop.

3. Double click on the Ready to Present folder.

4. Double click on the desired chapter.

5. Double click on the desired item.

Chapter 1

Putting It All Together:

Conducting Effective Staff

Development Workshops

Background and Information Needs

One of the primary responsibilities of today's school media specialist is to teach information literacy skills—not only to students but also to classroom teachers. With the introduction of new technologies in school media centers and classrooms the need for educators to integrate technology into the curriculum is being increasingly emphasized. In most situations a media specialist is not able to teach information skills to all the students in a school so help is needed from the classroom teachers. Unfortunately many classroom teachers are uncomfortable with the new technologies or have not had time to learn some of the information literacy skills themselves; thus, school media specialists can serve an important role by providing technology staff development workshops or programs to teachers. Of course, it is also important to remember that media specialists themselves are often overwhelmed with all the new technology that has become a part of their media centers or classrooms. As a result, many media specialists are in need of professional development workshops to become more comfortable with computers, the Internet, and other areas of technology as well as to learn how to teach the information literacy skills.

What Are the Needs?

The adage "Build it and they will come" from the film *The Field of Dreams* does not necessarily work with staff development for classroom teachers. "Conduct the presentation and they will come" is generally far from the truth. Classroom teachers are very busy, as are school media specialists, so if you want participants for a staff development program, you must first determine the technology or information literacy needs—as the teachers perceive them. This can be done informally at a faculty meeting, at department or grade level meetings, or by sending out a survey. Include suggestions about possible needs in your survey because some classroom teachers are not aware of how a piece of equipment or a computer software program might be helpful to them or to their students. Many teachers do not realize the importance of evaluating Web sites or are too embarrassed to tell you that they do not know how to use the new OPAC or how to use search engines. Be sure to keep their comfort levels in mind, no matter which method you use to determine their needs.

The next step might be to list all the expressed needs, and prioritize them according to the number of persons identifying a specific need. You will also want to consider how you and the school administration perceive the needs. For instance, perhaps teachers are violating copyright technology guidelines and this is a critical need that the administration would like to have addressed. After you have decided on the topic for the staff development program, you will then want to decide who is the best person to conduct the presentation.

Who Should Conduct a Staff Development Program?

It is almost impossible to be an "expert" in all areas of technology and information literacy. School personnel should not expect (although some do) that a media specialist be the "guru" in every facet of information literacy or technology. However, it is important for the school media specialist to have some familiarity with what technologies are available, how and when they should be used in educational settings, and the contribution they can make to effective student learning.

One idea for sharing the responsibility of teaching technology and information literacy skills is to divide up among media specialists some of the various areas of technology: digital cameras, video production, computer software, distance learning, Internet searching, copyright, Web design, presentation programs, electronic reading programs, networking, Web sites for different areas of the curriculum, etc. Then media specialists can develop one or more staff development programs in their areas of interest or expertise and be willing to share their presentations not only at their own schools, but also at other schools.

Often a classroom teacher may have expertise or interest in a particular area of technology. You, as a media specialist, should make a concerted effort to gather this type of information, either informally or through a survey. Even if classroom teachers are not willing to conduct entire programs on their own, they may be willing to help you plan or collaboratively conduct a staff development presentation. An extra person to help when it comes to hands-on activities for participants in an inservice workshop can be invaluable—and often makes the difference between successful and mediocre experiences for the participants.

Students should also be invited to help conduct staff development programs. Many of them have more expertise in areas of technology than anyone else in the school. Asking for their assistance makes good sense—and may keep some students from spending time hacking into computer programs and doing other mischievous tasks with a school's technology equipment. Again, as a media specialist you should never be timid about asking students for help with technology or teaching information skills to other students, not only in formal presentations, but in the daily routines of the media center. For many students, this experience can raise their self-esteem and give other students an opportunity to view these "techie" students in a positive light.

You will also want to utilize the talents of parent or community volunteers. Many of them have jobs in areas of technology or have special interests or hobbies that involve technology or information skills. They are often eager to share their technology or information literacy expertise in school settings.

If you live near a university or community college, you might also consider asking a professor or college instructor to conduct a workshop on a specific topic. Many university departments and educators have Web pages that describe faculty research and publication backgrounds, so it might be beneficial to consult those pages online. There are also several universities that maintain expertise speaker databases. Inviting a professor or instructor to conduct a staff development presentation, however, involves funding, so check with your school administrator for possible professional development monies. Also remember to ask the professor or instructor ahead of time what kind of fee would be charged and whether he or she has ever made such a presentation. Be prepared to tell him or her the number of expected participants and the length of time for the workshop. Also, be as specific as possible regarding your expectations and workshop objectives.

Vendors will often provide a consultant to conduct a workshop. If your need involves a specific piece of equipment or a software program your school is purchasing or has recently purchased, check with a company representative and see what type of arrangements can be made. Sometimes the company will send someone for gratis but other times a charge will be involved. So again, be aware of available funding and be specific about what is needed in the way of a staff development workshop.

How Is the Planning Done?

 Length of the Program

Planning is undoubtedly the most important and time-consuming step in conducting a workshop. If you are conducting the program, one of the first things you want to consider is how best to fulfill the need expressed by your participants. Some needs, such as how to operate a piece of equipment (for example, a scanner, digital camera, or video camera), are what can be considered "one-shot" staff development presentations in which the material can be covered in perhaps an hour or two. Evaluating Web sites or learning to search an OPAC are other topics that can be addressed in one-shot programs.

Other types of needs are best addressed in a half-day or all-day workshop. Such topics include learning a presentation program like PowerPoint or creating and editing a digital video. For this type of staff development workshop, present part of the material, give participants an opportunity to use that skill, and then move on to the next skill until participants have a fairly complete understanding of the skills and are able to create at least a simple product. You do not need to teach all the intricacies of PowerPoint or designing a Web page, but you do want to provide the participants with enough information and motivation for them to continue experimenting and learning.

Other topics are best presented in a series of workshops. These include more complex topics or topics in which you want the participants to apply or think about the knowledge gained during the time between each session. An example is the possible introduction of an electronic reading program, such as Reading Counts or Accelerated Reader, into a school curriculum. The initial session might be used for an overview of the program, discussion of some of the controversies about the program, ideas on how best to implement the program, and perhaps an introduction to some Web sites and articles on the topic that can be read by the participants before the next session. If faculty members decide to proceed with the idea of an electronic reading program, other sessions might include taking a more thorough look at the program itself and how it works, trying out some of the tests that accompany the program, and discussing how the program will be implemented in the school. After the program is actually being used in the classrooms or in the media center, teachers will benefit from a staff development presentation to address any problems or concerns that either they or their students may be having with the program. In an additional session you might want to focus on the evaluation of the electronic reading program in relation to student reading progress or motivation to see if teachers want to continue or alter the use of the electronic reading program.

 Getting Participants to Attend

Staff development programs can be voluntary or mandatory (if so designated by the administration). If your presentation is going to be voluntary it is still important to get the support of school administrators. If teachers think the principal expects them to attend or if the principal lets it be known that he or she is going to be present at the program, teachers will be more likely to attend. One useful technique is to ask an administrator to announce the staff development presentation and encourage teachers to attend.

Other incentives for attendance are providing continuing education points, college credit, or a small honorarium if funding is available. Providing refreshments or a free lunch will also encourage attendees.

Sending out creative invitations that announce the topic, time, and place of the presentation is a great way to encourage attendance. Some media specialists also include an RSVP so they can prepare for a certain number of attendees. Strategically placed flyers or posters will serve as reminders—as will announcements on a school listserv or over the school intercom.

It is also important to take into consideration the time you offer the workshop. Most teachers prefer an after-school meeting if the program is no longer than 90 minutes. Of course, Friday after school is never a good day to schedule a meeting. For longer workshops (a half-day or all-day), a day in the summer is a possibility.

However, you may run into difficulty publicizing your staff development program if you wait too far into summer vacation. Some media specialists report having success with Saturday workshops, but more media specialists seem to have difficulty getting attendees on a Saturday since many teachers are involved with their families. If you are in a middle school or high school, you might want to try scheduling several smaller staff development opportunities during teachers' planning periods.

? Deciding on Activities

Before you decide what activities to include in your staff development program, you need to identify your objectives. What is it you would like your participants to learn from the workshop? At what level do you expect the teachers to be able to perform a skill at the end of your program?

After you have identified the objectives, plan for the activities that will be most effective in reaching those objectives. It is a good idea to begin with a general background about the technology and its significance. How can the technology help the teachers? Has there been any meaningful research relating to the topic? Do you know of some examples that illustrate the importance of the topic? You want to keep this part of the program relatively short, but it is essential for teachers to have some general understanding of the topic.

Although your presentation may necessitate some lecture, try to keep a good balance between lecture, demonstration, and hands-on activities. For instance, if you want to teach your participants how to use a scanner, you could begin by giving a short lecture about the background and possible uses of scanners in the curriculum. Then, move on to demonstrating the scanner, and finally provide each participant with an opportunity to scan a photo or a short page of text. You should consider ahead of time how to divide participants into groups for activities. Also, identify who can help provide needed assistance during hands-on activities.

Preparing the Materials

Be sure to have all your materials prepared before the presentation. Check out all the equipment ahead of time to make certain everything is working properly. Be aware of troubleshooting tips that might assist you if you experience difficulty with a piece of equipment. If possible, have back-up equipment available. Even though you might have bulbs available when one burns out of an overhead or slide projector, it is usually much faster to have another piece of equipment set up and ready if needed. When working with technology it is also important to have some back-up materials available. For instance, if you are relying on a PowerPoint presentation for a lecture, make transparencies of the presentation in case you experience computer problems.

If your participants need materials for a hands-on activity, place the materials, as well as an agenda and handouts, at each table or computer station to save time. It is always a good idea to have extra pens, pencils, scrap paper, and paper clips available. Another effective way of managing materials is to provide them in a pocketed folder for each participant. Using different color paper for the handouts makes it easier for participants to locate an item in the folder when it is needed. For instance, you can ask participating teachers to remove the yellow page from the folder for a specific list of directions.

For some workshops, it is especially helpful to create electronic folders for each participant ahead of time. The folders should contain images, documents, or templates that will facilitate the activities. For example, the folder could contain pre-selected holiday images from which the participants could choose to create a holiday card. This will save time and keep all participants on task.

If you are providing refreshments, make certain you have ordered or prepared them ahead of time. Confirmation order reminders on the day before the staff development presentation are a good idea if someone else is preparing the refreshments.

Provide plenty of set-up time for your program so you will be both physically and mentally prepared for the teachers as they arrive. If you are pressed for time, having students or volunteer parents help you with the set up can be extremely beneficial so you can be mentally relaxed to conduct the program.

How Should the Staff Development Workshop Be Conducted?

 Creature Comforts

"Creature comforts" can contribute to an effective staff development presentation. Making certain the room temperature is appropriate for the group might take some advance preparation, particularly if you are in a room in which you are not able to directly control the air conditioning or heating. It will be very difficult for participants to concentrate on the topic of the program if they are trying to stay warm or if perspiration is rolling down their backs. If the workshop is longer than two hours, try to arrange for a room with comfortable chairs, rather than the typical student desk chairs. Using a few festive decorations that match the theme of the program will help get the participants thinking about the topic and will create a pleasant, welcoming atmosphere. If participants are coming to a location that is not familiar to them, provide driving directions and post signs from the main door of the building.

Try to provide some type of refreshments for the participants. This might not be possible if the workshop is being held in a computer lab or a room where food is off-limits. However, if the program is being held after school, or if participants are driving a long way to attend, they will appreciate having refreshing drinks and a choice of both sweet and non-sweet snacks available upon arrival. Let your participants know in your invitations or publicity flyers that refreshments will be served. In planning your agenda, remember to include a short time for socialization, preferably before the formal presentation begins. Providing clean, well-stocked restrooms may also take some advance preparation.

Managing the Participants

As anyone who has conducted a staff development activity might tell you, managing a group of teachers can be just as challenging as managing a classroom of elementary or teenage students. In fact, sometimes it can be more difficult if the teachers want to talk and socialize, rather than learn about the topic. For this reason, it is important to have an agenda for the participants, as well as a carefully designed plan for the activities. Try to begin on time, stick to the agenda, and complete the program at the designated time. Providing handouts captures attention, helps teach a skill and also keeps the participants on task.

When working with technology you will need to consider the various levels of skill and experience that the participants have with a particular type of technology. It may be advantageous to informally survey the teachers and ask them to rate themselves as beginner, intermediate, or advanced. Then, when you provide some time for hands-on activities, such as editing a short video production, you can include an intermediate or advanced skilled participant in each group. If you are in a computer lab, seating the participants so a beginner is next to someone with more computer skills is extremely beneficial. Teachers often spontaneously help one another, but you may need to suggest to the more advanced-skilled participants that they work with their peers who need some assistance.

Providing some type of demonstration (and not just lecture) is especially helpful to your participants. If you are demonstrating a piece of equipment, make certain that everyone is able to see. Having more than one piece of the equipment and using additional helpers (perhaps students or teachers) will make the demonstration even more effective. Once a demonstration is complete, it is important for every participant to have the opportunity to have hands-on experiences. For instance, if you are demonstrating a digital camera, have more than one camera available and let every participant take at least one photo and download it to a computer. Whenever you are able to include a make-and-take it activity, the chances that participants will follow up on the skill are significantly increased. Other ideas for make-and-take projects include asking teachers to bring at least one photo to a workshop and learn to scan it or asking teachers to bring one of their upcoming lessons to a workshop and have them make a PowerPoint presentation to use in the lesson.

Remember to be patient with your participants; it's as important as being patient with students. Encourage them, and try to empathize with any feelings of discomfort they may be experiencing. Additionally, showing a good sense of humor goes a long way in putting both you and the participants at ease. Providing some type of reward at the end of a workshop is also appropriate. Perhaps a certificate for having learned a skill can be presented to each participant. Teachers also love door prizes. You might want to align the door prizes to the theme of your presentation by giving a book or poster about technology or perhaps an unusual mouse pad. Even if the door prizes have nothing to do with the workshop itself, participants generally enjoy receiving them.

Evaluation

Every staff development presentation should have an evaluation, whether it is formal or informal. When planning for your program you need to consider the type of evaluation you will use. The evaluation should refer back to the objectives of the presentation and assist you in determining whether the objectives were accomplished. Short surveys, questioning the participants, or viewing the participants' finished products can help you make judgments about how successful you were in accomplishing your specified objectives. If you ask teachers to fill out a brief survey, you might also want to include a few questions relating to the effectiveness of your presentation or the usefulness of the information and provide a means of making suggestions for improvement of future workshops. The survey should be one page or less in length and take no more than five minutes to complete. You will receive more honest responses if you allow for the surveys to be anonymous and provide a place, such as a basket or box, where the evaluations can be turned in, rather than handed to you.

Follow-Up Activities

Even though the presentation portion of your staff development program is complete, you will still want to do some follow-up activities. First, you should encourage the teachers to continue working with the technology or information literacy skills you presented. You can offer to meet with the teachers individually or set up some small groups where the teachers can work together on projects. If equipment is needed, be certain to let teachers know that you will make the equipment available to them at certain times so they can continue practicing or developing products. Check with teachers either individually or on the school listserv to see if they would like you to provide them with additional support. Consider making an Internet tutorial to provide assistance. Also be sure to offer a time at future faculty or department meetings when teachers can share their success stories relating to the technology topic.

An additional follow-up activity includes sending thank you notes to volunteers or donors. A short report about the program can also be a beneficial tool. It can be sent to administrators or kept on file for your evaluation.

Final Tips

☑ Constantly be attuned to teacher needs for topic ideas.

☑ Prepare, prepare, prepare. Practice, practice, practice.

☑ Learn from your evaluations; strive to improve.

☑ Be proactive; seek opportunities to help your teachers.

☑ Share your talents at conferences.

Chapter 2

Don't Be a Copy Cat:

Learning About Copyright

Background and Information Needs

What staff development topic is most needed by educators? As former school media specialists, our answer would be copyright, particularly as it relates to the new technologies. Unfortunately, some educators are not aware of this need or do not want to hear about it. This was one author's experience fifteen years ago when she was hired as a media specialist in a public high school. At least half the videos in the media center collection were illegal copies made by the previous media specialist—at the direction of a principal and social studies teacher. It took a large amount of educating by the new media specialist to convince the principal and teachers at that school of the importance of following copyright laws and guidelines. Fortunately, today many administrators and school districts have become more aware of the need for developing copyright policies and for copyright education.

Copyright laws and guidelines have always had a reputation of being confusing. With the advent of new technologies—copy machines, videocassettes, computer software, DVDs, scanners, Internet, digitizers, and MP3 files (a compressed audio format for obtaining and distributing music from CDs), copyright issues have become even more complicated. Consequently, it is essential that educators become informed on the topic.

In many schools media specialists are responsible for keeping current on copyright issues and educating teachers and students. An informal survey of LM-NET and EDTECH discussion list users indicated that the school librarian is the primary person for informing students and teachers about copyright and other cyberethics issues. Even the computer teachers, who noted that they tried to include copyright in their lessons, named the school librarian as the campus leader in this area (Bell, 2002). Being in such a position has become difficult for some media specialists who feel "caught in-between." While they have worked hard to align themselves with teachers and be supportive, media specialists placed in this role do not always win popularity contests, particularly if administrators expect media specialists to monitor for copyright infringements. Thus, it is essential that, as a media specialist, you clarify your administrator's expectations of you with regard to copyright. Our advice to you is to not act as a copyright policeman, nor even give advice to teachers. Rather, you should provide the copyright information that teachers need. An administrator should deal with any violations of copyright or possible confrontations—except if the infringements are happening in the media center or on equipment owned by the media center. In those cases, you become a liable party. Finding a balance in your role with regard to copyright issues is important. While a media specialist should work within the spirit of the copyright law, it is also your job to protect patrons' rights to use and share information whenever possible (Russell, 2001).

If a copyright policy is not in place in your district or school, it is advisable for you to assertively encourage and take active leadership in the development of such a policy. Examples of policies can be found online. One of the most important aspects of a policy is the assignment of responsibilities. It should be the responsibility of all district employees to be knowledgeable about and comply with copyright law. The school media specialist can be assigned to disseminate information about copyright, but the responsibility of enforcing compliance is most appropriately assigned to administrators (generally the principal at the building level). Statements placing the liability for infringement upon the person in violation of the copyright laws should be included in the policy to protect the institution and other school employees. Additionally, the consequences of violating the policy should also be included. Legal counsel should always approve the final draft of a policy. Once a copyright policy is in place and it is ready to be implemented, school employees will more readily acknowledge their need for staff development on the topic.

Before conducting staff development on copyright, you must first educate your-self on the subject. This can be done by reading books and journal articles (some journals have regular columns devoted to copyright issues), attending conferences or workshops, or accessing some of the numerous Web sites on the topic. There are also helpful tutorials on the Internet; however, it is important to evaluate the information source and select only reputable sites. We have listed what we consider to be valuable copyright resources later in this chapter.

What Is Copyright?

One of the first concepts that you will want to learn is the definition of copyright. "Copyright can best be described as a statutory privilege extended to the creators of works which are fixed in a tangible medium of expression" (Jackson, 1991, p. 31). The statutory privilege referred to in this definition is the 1976 copyright law found in Title 17 of the *U.S. Code*. Tangible mediums of expression include items such as books, audiocassettes, videocassettes, music scores, journal articles, DVDs, and computer software—items that can be touched. The purpose of this 1978 law is to give the creators of intellectual properties (authors, poets, illustrators, music composers, video and software producers, etc.) the right to determine when and how their works are to be used for a particular length of time. All works created on or after January 1, 1978 are protected by copyright and do not necessarily need the symbol ©. After the period of copyright protection expires, the material is then in public domain and the material can be used in any manner desired. More information related to public domain can be found at <//www.copyright.iupui.edu/permitintro.htm>.

In 1998, the U.S. Congress passed the Digital Millennium Copyright Act (DMCA). The law is complex, but most would agree that the DMCA places even tighter controls over access to and use of copyrighted materials. Many of these changes in copyright law are being challenged in court so we can probably expect to see even more changes and interpretations of the law in the next several years (Russell, 2001).

Because of severe copyright limitations on what could be shown or performed using distant education technologies, Congress passed the TEACH Act in late 2002. This act expanded the scope of educators' rights to perform and display works and to make copies that are integral to such performances and displays for digital distance education. The TEACH Act thus made the rights for distance education closer to those in face-to-face instruction (Harper, 2002).

What Is Fair Use?

Section 107 of Title 17 of the *U.S. Code* provides factors to be considered in determining whether the use of a copyrighted work is "fair use." Those factors include:

- the purpose and character of the use, including whether such use is of a commercial nature or is for nonprofit educational purposes;
- the nature of the copyrighted work;
- the amount and substantiality of the portion used in relation to the copyrighted work as a whole; and,
- the effect of the use upon the potential market for or value of the copyrighted work.

The purpose of limited exceptions of the exclusive rights of copyright owners is to advance knowledge and scholarship. Thus, this section of the law is particularly important to the educational community. The language of the law, however, is very brief and vague. Both houses of the U.S. Congress held committee hearings to provide guidelines for the interpretation of the copyright law and to try to determine an equitable balance between the rights of copyright owners and those of the general public. These guidelines are often referred to as the "Congressional Guidelines" or the "Fair Use Guidelines." The guidelines provide quite explicit recommendations about the amounts and types of copying that can be considered "fair use" (Simpson, 2001). The complete guidelines can be found at <http://library.lp.findlaw.com/articles/00059/003456.pdf>. Although these guidelines from Congressionally appointed committees help answer many questions about photocopying, off-air videotaping, and music copying, educators have been forced to make judgment calls on other types of copies made from the newer technologies.

What Types of Information Should Be Included in a Workshop?

The types of copyright information to include in this staff development presentation depend on the audience. There are topics that are more specific to higher education institutions (such as the development of course packets containing copyrighted materials), to librarians (such as interlibrary loan restrictions), to classroom teachers in K-12 settings (such as amounts of materials that can be photocopied) or to students (such as the types and amounts of materials that can be included in a student multimedia presentation). If you are presenting an initial workshop to personnel in a K-12 setting, you should address the topics that are most valuable to that audience. The types of technology that are present in a school will also influence the amount of time you spend on particular topics. For instance, if distance learning is occurring in a school, this topic needs to be addressed in your staff development workshop. The workshop we have developed on copyright is a general one intended for K-12 personnel who have fairly limited knowledge on copyright. You may want to adjust the workshop to the needs and sophistication of your particular audience.

Planning

Once you have been sufficiently educated on copyright law and guidelines (few of us are experts in this area), you can begin planning a staff development workshop on the subject. Because of the topic's complexity, this is one workshop where you might want to obtain the assistance of others whom you consider to be more knowledgeable about copyright. Perhaps they can review the information you plan to present in your workshop. You might even want to consider having a lawyer attend the workshop to answers questions. There might be a parent of a child in the school who is a lawyer familiar with copyright or the school district may permit you to have the district's counsel present or available by phone for questions at the end of the workshop. It is important for you to acknowledge your limitations regarding copyright knowledge, and yet also let the audience know that you are trying to help them by providing information about the topic.

 Length of Time

The basics of copyright can probably be addressed in a single, 60 to 90 minute presentation. Copyright is a very complex topic so it is not possible to address all the aspects in one session. However, the subject can become tedious for some participants, especially if they are learning about all the restrictions to their instructional activities; thus, we would not recommend beginning with a full-day workshop on the topic. After an initial presentation, other workshop opportunities can be offered, depending upon need and interest. Providing additional print and online resources on copyright is essential.

 Materials and Equipment

A large amount of equipment is not needed to present the information for this workshop. However, if you want to have hands-on activities where participants explore copyright Web sites, consider having computers with Internet access available.

This workshop lends itself well to a pre-test of the participants' copyright knowledge; developing a one-page "test" that can be filled out during the first few minutes of the workshop is a good way to focus the participants' attention on the topic. The pre-test is not something you want to grade. Rather, it should contain questions relating to the information you are going to present in the workshop. Participants can then compare their knowledge to the workshop information and continue to learn throughout the presentation.

 ## Getting Participants

Teachers, administrators, and paraprofessionals all need to be informed about copyright law and guidelines. In many schools, paraprofessionals are working in the computer labs or as assistants in school media centers. Often their responsibilities deal directly with activities that are affected by copyright; so it is important that they be included in any staff development that deals with this topic. If at all possible, you should try to make the workshop mandatory. The best way to do this is to have administrators support the workshop and make announcements dealing with their expectations of attendance. Be prepared to have some participants show possible resentment if attendance at the workshop is mandatory. Being upbeat and concentrating on how the workshop will help the participants and their students will hopefully lessen any negative feelings.

Flyers or invitations that provide information about the workshop should be sent out as early as possible, particularly if the staff development is mandatory. If the workshop is not mandatory, request an RSVP. Make certain that the workshop will be held in a location that will comfortably seat all attendees.

 ## Deciding on Activities

Possible overall goals for this workshop are to help participants become more knowledgeable about copyright issues and to encourage their adherence, and that of their students, to copyright laws and guidelines. Objectives for the participants of the staff development session might include the following:

- Define copyright and its background
- Define public domain
- Identify materials that are protected by copyright
- Identify copyright owners' rights
- Define fair use and identify examples of fair use
- Verbalize reasons for following copyright guidelines
- Identify means of following copyright guidelines

When you have determined your objectives, you will be ready to plan some activities to meet those objectives. We have developed a PowerPoint presentation that can assist you in doing so. You may want to alter parts of the presentation to fit the needs of your audience and school.

Preparing the Materials

Before you begin the workshop, check the equipment that will be needed to show your PowerPoint slides. The following materials should be available for the participants:

- An agenda
- A pre-test relating to copyright knowledge
- A handout of the PowerPoint presentation, with three slides per page and space for the participants to take notes during the workshop
- A handout listing resources for copyright information
- Computers for the participants to access Web sites
- A handout of a sample form that can be used to ask for copyright permission
- An evaluation form

Try putting up some decorations using a "copy cat" theme. A few posters or a bulletin board featuring cats might help participants become comfortable with the focus of the workshop. Be creative and perhaps you can also come up with ideas for refreshments in the same theme—maybe those Halloween cat cookies available at bakeries or cut out with cookie cutters.

Conducting the Workshop

After participants have enjoyed the refreshments, direct them to tables where you have placed pencils and PowerPoint handouts for each individual. Wait until all participants are ready, and then announce that you would like them to take a pre-test of their knowledge about copyright. Assure them that the test will not be graded, and that they can change any of their answers as you move through your staff development presentation. Then distribute the pre-tests and ask the participants to complete them within ten minutes, without talking to other individuals at their tables.

When the pre-test activity is complete, move immediately into the PowerPoint presentation, beginning with information dealing with copyright definition and some of the fair use guidelines. When you come to the slides dealing with scenarios, pause after each scenario before showing the slide with the correct response and let the participants at each table discuss the scenario. Ask representatives from some of the tables to report back their answers. If time is short, you may want to vary this activity by sometimes having the participants raise their hands to respond to the question asked in each scenario. After participants have responded, then show the slide with the correct response. Remember to praise the participants when a majority of them have selected the correct responses. Also, ask the participants if they have questions about the scenarios.

When you have completed discussing the scenarios, direct the participants to the slide in their PowerPoint handout that lists selected resources on copyright information. Divide the participants into groups and assign each group a Web site to explore. Suggest that they take notes relating to anything they find that is new information. After ten minutes of site exploration, ask participants to return to tables, where they can briefly share some of the information they learned.

When the discussions are complete, direct the participants' attention to the handout that includes a form for requesting copyright permission. Encourage participants to make use of the form and assure them that authors and other creators of intellectual property are often generous about sharing their material for educational purposes.

Before distributing an evaluation, ask the teachers for their ideas on how to share the information that they learned with their students. Encourage them to follow through with some of these ideas in their classrooms.

Evaluation

 Evaluation for this activity should focus on whether the participants gained knowledge about copyright, whether they understand the importance of adhering to copyright law and guidelines, and whether they will participate in activities to share copyright information with their students. Remember that participants should not have to sign their names to the evaluations.

Follow-Up Activities

You will want to make certain that participants have opportunities to continue to receive copyright information. The book, *Copyright for Schools: A Practical Guide* (Linworth, 2001) is easy to understand and should be a part of every school's professional collection. Directing workshop participants to this resource, as well as to other materials, such as a file of journal articles dealing with copyright, will make it possible for participants to further their copyright education.

A suggested follow-up activity to the workshop is viewing a copyright video at a faculty meeting. Even though some of the same material may be covered in a video, this will help reinforce the information. The Association for Information Media and Equipment (AIME) has videos for this purpose. Annotations of AIME resources can be found at <http://www.aime.org/resources.php>.

A couple of weeks after the workshop, e-mail participants to find out if any of them have developed lessons to teach their students about copyright. If so, ask those teachers if they are willing to share their lessons at an upcoming faculty meeting.

An additional means of educating teachers and students about copyright is to make a brochure that can be distributed to all teachers and students. Students might also try their hands at developing creative brochures with copyright information, but be sure the information is reviewed for accuracy before any brochures are distributed.

Final Tips

☑ Don't be afraid to address copyright as an ethical, as well as a legal, issue.

☑ Suggest to your administrator that all teachers and staff members sign a copyright compliance agreement.

☑ Keep current on copyright issues.

☑ And finally, it is essential that you be a model for copyright compliance in all your professional activities.

References

Bell, Mary Ann. (2002). Cyberethics in schools: What is going on? *Book Report, 21* (1), 33-35.

Harper, Georgia. (2002). *The TEACH Act finally becomes law.* Retrieved on October 31, 2003, from <http://www.utsystem.edu/ogc/intellectualproperty/ teachact.htm>

Jackson, Mary E. (1991). Copyright, libraries & media centers. *Media & Methods, 27* (3), 34-37.

Russell, Carrie. (2001). Stolen words. *School Library Journal, 47* (2), 40-43.

Simpson, Carol (2001). *Copyright for schools: A practical guide* (3rd ed.). Worthington, OH: Linworth.

Selected Resources

Books

Hoffman, Gretchen McCord. (2001). *Copyright in cyberspace: Questions and answers for librarians.* New York: Neal-Schumann.

This book serves as a basic guide to copyright laws and fair use guidelines as they relate to the cyber world. The author's presentation leads readers to further explore copyright issues.

Simpson, Carol. (2001). *Copyright for schools: A practical guide.* Worthington, OH: Linworth.

A must for all schools, this book provides easy-to-understand information on a variety of copyright issues, including fair use, print works, electronic formats, and distance learning. The appendix contains several helpful items, such as important Internet links and a reproducible brochure.

United States Copyright Office. (1995). *Circular 21: Reproduction of copyrighted works by educators and librarians.* Washington, DC: Library of Congress, Copyright Office.

This 22-page booklet has information relating to reproduction of copyrighted materials for educators at all levels, as well as for libraries and archives. Exclusive rights, fair use, excerpts from the 1975 Senate Report, the 1976 House Report, and the 1976 Conference Report, liability for infringement, and guidelines for off-air recording of broadcast programming for educational purposes are included. The booklet is also available in pdf format from: <http://library.lp.findlaw.com/articles/00059/003456.pdf>

Web Sites

American Library Association. (2003). *Copyright issues*. Retrieved April 15, 2003, from <http://www.ala.org/content/NavigationMenu/Our_Association/offices/ALA_Washington/Issues2/Copyright1/Copyright.htm>

This Web site, one of several sponsored by ALA, provides information on the status of copyright issues that ALA tracks every day. Links to other copyright topics, such as UCITA, court cases, distance education, the Digital Millennium Copyright Act (DMCA), and articles are provided at the beginning of the site.

Copyright website. (2002). Retrieved March 20, 2003, from <http://www.benedict.com/default.asp>

This award-winning, well-designed site serves as a portal for much practical copyright information.

Indiana University. (2002). *Copyright management center*. Retrieved April 15, 2003, from <http://www.copyright.iupui.edu/>

The basics of copyright information, fair-use issues, copyright permission information, and copyright ownership are among the topics addressed on this site.

Joseph, Linda C. (2002). *Copyright with Cyberbee*. Retrieved March 20, 2003, from <http://www.cyberbee.com/copyrt.html>

Young students can use this site to find copyright information. A fun, interactive quiz and a copyright lesson plan are included, as well as links to other helpful sites.

Library of Congress.(2003). *United States Copyright Office*. Retrieved April 14, 2003, from <http://lcweb.loc.gov/copyright/>

All copyright registration forms (many in fill-in format) and all informational circulars are available at this Web site, which is the official copyright office at the Library of Congress. The ability to search copyright registrations and recorded documents from 1978 is also available, as well as a frequently asked questions segment.

O'Mahoney, Benedict. (2002). *About copyright Website LLC*. Retrieved April 14, 2003, from <http://www.benedict. com/home/resume/copyrightwebsite.asp>

The site is designed to facilitate the copyright registration process via the computer through the use of its Copyright Wizard.

Materials Available on the Accompanying CD-ROM

- Flyer (Book Marks)
- Agenda
- Copyright Pretest
- PowerPoint Presentation

- Selected Resources Handout
- Sample Form for Copyright Permission
- Evaluation

Chapter 3

The Plagiarism Plague:

Detection and Prevention

Background and Information Needs

Academic dishonesty in student work is not a new issue in schools, but with the introduction of Internet access, the problem has become nearly epidemic. Cutting and pasting from Web pages, using material without citing sources, and purchasing research papers from online "paper mills" to complete written assignments have become commonplace examples of student plagiarism. Bushweller (1999) noted that in a nationwide survey of 356 teachers, nine out of ten high school teachers reported that cheating was a problem in their schools, while almost as many said an increasing number of students were plagiarizing information from the Internet. In a Rutgers University study that surveyed 4,500 students from 25 high schools, 72 percent of the respondents indicated they had cheated on at least one written assignment and 57 percent of the students said they did not think copying a few sentences without giving appropriate credit to the source was actually cheating (Sorokin, 2002). Addressing the problem of student plagiarism is not simple or straightforward. Students need to understand what actually constitutes plagiarism and how to avoid it in their assignments. They also need to be taught the related ethics. Additionally, teachers should be educated in ways to help prevent student plagiarism.

Most people tend to think that the responsibility of educating students about plagiarism lies with classroom teachers; however, media specialists can and should help support teachers in this task. Standard 8 of the school media specialists' Information Literacy Standards, *Information Power: Building Partnerships for Learning* states "The student who contributes positively to the learning community and to society is information literate and practices ethical behavior in regard to information and information technology" (AASL & AECT, 1998, p. 36). The guidelines go on to list indicators of attainment of this standard:

> Students understand the concept of fair use and apply it, they recognize and diligently avoid plagiarism, they follow an information-seeking process to come to their own conclusions, they express their conclusions in their own words rather than copying the conclusions or arguments presented by others, and they follow bibliographic form and cite all information sources used (p. 37).

These statements from the national standards indicate that school media specialists should be concerned about the ethical use of information. Many school media specialists have fought for copyright adherence in schools, but what are they doing to help prevent student plagiarism? In his article, "Copyright's (Not So) Little Cousin, Plagiarism," D. Scott Brandt (2002) notes that copyright and plagiarism are closely related, and both deserve the attention of librarians. Educating teachers and students about plagiarism can also provide excellent collaborative opportunities for media specialists and classroom teachers. Media specialists who offer educators workshops about plagiarism can also work together with teachers to design creative lessons that will help prevent plagiarism.

What Is Plagiarism?

Simply stated, plagiarism is using another person's ideas or words without clearly acknowledging the source of the information. We most often think of plagiarism in terms of the written word, but it also can involve the spoken word, as well as graphs, drawings, or figures. Students need to understand that plagiarism involves both theft and lying—it is taking someone else's words and ideas and passing them off as one's own. Although in this chapter we are discussing plagiarism as it relates to students and education, plagiarism is, unfortunately, fairly rampant in other areas of our society. The highly respected newspaper *The New York Times* recently had instances of well-known reporters failing to provide appropriate credit to portions of their news stories, which resulted in the reporters' resignations, as well as the resignations of the paper's two top editors. These incidences sparked debates relating to plagiarism and sloppiness in American journalism.

Why Do Students Cheat on Papers?

In some instances, such as not citing information appropriately, students do not intentionally plagiarize written assignments; they simply do not understand what constitutes plagiarism and how to avoid it. However, if papers are copied or purchased from Internet sites or "borrowed" from friends, there is little doubt that the plagiarism is deliberate. Why do students cheat on written assignments? The following are a few possible reasons:

- The belief that it is normal, common behavior
- Pressure for good grades or fear of bad grades
- Poor time management skills or procrastination
- Being involved in too many activities
- Fear that their writing and research skills are inadequate
- Laziness
- Peer pressure
- The thrill of getting away with it
- Temptation—it is easy to do
- Lack of interest in the research topic

How Can We Educate Students About Plagiarism?

In order to educate students about plagiarism, we must not only explain what plagiarism is, but also explain why it is wrong and how to avoid it. Showing examples of plagiarism is an excellent way to help students understand the concepts involved. Plagiarism examples can include not giving credit to: (1) another person's direct words, (2) another person's ideas or opinions, (3) facts or statistics, or (4) the paraphrasing of another person's spoken or written words. After examples are used to clarify these issues, a teacher should then present lessons that show students how to properly cite in each of the instances.

A classroom discussion relating to ethics and plagiarism is essential. Reasons for student cheating should be included in this conversation. As previously mentioned, many students do not think plagiarism is wrong. Thus, one should be ready to address the attitudes and examples that students will most likely bring to such a discussion, including possible differences in familial and cultural views. Educators should talk to students about intellectual property rights—their own as well as others' rights. Without a discussion of plagiarism and ethics it is likely that students will not truly understand why plagiarism should be avoided. Consequently, this lack of information could contribute to the attitude of "It is okay as long as I don't get caught." Technology has made it fairly simple for many students to "get away" with plagiarism. Instead of thinking that we can catch all student plagiarism, educators need to try to promote honorable, ethical attitudes toward student work. Asking students who is really being cheated when someone plagiarizes can spark an interesting dialogue. If possible, some type of action should follow classroom discussion. Asking students to help develop and implement an academic honesty policy that includes plagiarism is an excellent means of actively involving students in this issue.

According to an article in *U.S. News and World Report* (Kleiner & Lord, 1999), one of the primary reasons plagiarism thrives is the lack of consequences. Teachers should be aware of any academic honesty policies that exist in their schools. If no such policy exists, they, along with the media specialist, should work to institute such a policy. It is important for students to be informed of the consequences of plagiarism. In addition to announcing the consequences to a class, the penalties should be clearly written into the policy. The stated penalties or consequences for plagiarism not only may help prevent some students from being tempted to plagiarize, but they also reassure honest students that their work efforts are respected.

How Can Teachers Identify and Prevent Plagiarism?

One of the most important ways that teachers can identify and prevent plagiarism is to become familiar with the technology that makes it possible for students to easily plagiarize their assignments. There are several Web sites that give away or sell term papers to students. Some of these are listed at the end of this chapter. Teachers should access the sites that are commonly referred to as "paper mills," see what types of materials are available, and then avoid the topics that are listed.

Students can also use the Internet to cheat on a written assignment by typing a subject into a search engine, finding pages with information on the topic, and then cutting and pasting text into a word processing program. One way to prevent this is for teachers to become familiar with search engines that are often used by students. Google, Yahoo, and AskJeeves are three such search engines. Using those search engines, teachers can then perform their own searches to determine if student papers contain instances of plagiarism. No search engine retrieves all items on the Internet so it is advisable to use more than one search engine. Meta-search engines, such as ProFusion, qbSearch, Dogpile, and Excite, all of which access multiple search engines, can be useful for this purpose. Taking an unusual phrase from a student's paper and submitting it to a search will usually result in finding the original source fairly quickly. Requiring students to hand in electronic versions of their assignments can make this searching even easier since a teacher can then cut and paste phrases into a search engine to see if there are items online that match.

More sophisticated software programs and search services can also be used to detect plagiarism. Turnitin.com, EVE2 (easy verification engine), and GLATT Plagiarism Service are some examples. All of these programs and services must be purchased, but in some instances free online trials are provided. It is important to be aware of the shortcomings of plagiarism detection services; they should be viewed only as tools to assist educators in trying to determine whether plagiarism has taken place.

Often a teacher may have gut feelings that a paper is "too good" to be a particular student's work. While heeding those feelings, educators should also be aware of signs that might indicate instances of plagiarism. Such signs include:

- Absence of references
- Absence of current references
- Mixed styles of references, such as APA with MLA
- Quotes without references
- Numerous bibliographic sources to which the school does not have access
- Advanced vocabulary or sentence structure
- Mixed styles of writing, such as journalistic with scholarly
- Inconsistent formatting of margins, headings, or fonts
- Gray letters in the text which indicate the text may have appeared in a different color font on a Web page
- Other telltale indications of information that appears on Web pages, such as a URL at the top or bottom of a page

- Inactive Web sites listed in the references
- Irrelevant information
- Inappropriate use of figures of speech

One of the most effective ways to prevent plagiarism is for educators to redesign assignments. Instead of asking for facts, McKenzie (1998) recommends emphasizing assignments that challenge students to utilize the higher thinking skills at the top of Bloom's taxonomy. In doing so, students move from mere gathering of facts to construction of new meanings and insights.

Additionally, by requiring products other than the usual written report or research paper, the chances of plagiarism decrease. Cummings (2003) presents some ideas for alternative research products: writing e-mails or postcards home about life in a location that the student has researched, creating a travel brochure on a biome, writing research findings in a story format, or researching information to respond to a situational activity. Asking students to orally present their topics, limiting students' use of reference sources to the past few years, requiring students to provide personal opinions, and having students write reflective summaries of their research are additional strategies to prevent student plagiarism. Making very specific assignments and listing relevant topics from which students must make selections also reduces opportunities for plagiarism.

Another means of minimizing plagiarism is requiring process steps in which a preliminary bibliography, outline, rough draft, research materials (copies of articles and other sources), final draft, and annotated bibliography are built into the assignment (Harris, 2002). Having students write a short, in-class essay about what they learned from the assignment also helps identify student work that warrants further investigation.

Once students realize that their teachers are familiar with paper mill sites and know how to search for plagiarized assignments and check into any questionable sources, the chances of plagiarism can be drastically reduced. It is always important to remember when dealing with plagiarism that the burden of proof lies with the educator. Before addressing a possible case of plagiarism, it is wise to gather all possible documentation and share it with an administrator. Unfortunately, there are cases when, even though plagiarism is proven, administrators, parents, or school boards may not support the consequences. However, if we as educators do not take active roles in the prevention of plagiarism, we will undoubtedly watch it continue to flourish in our educational institutions.

What Should You Include in a Workshop?

Before presenting a workshop on plagiarism, you may want to survey classroom teachers to determine their attitudes, concerns, and experiences as they relate to student cheating in their classrooms. Consider including some questions about the teachers' knowledge of ways students plagiarize and how it can be prevented. The survey responses can provide you with ideas about what to include in a staff development program. The make-up of the audience (middle school or high school teachers, specific or mixed subject area teachers) will also help you with this task. Minimally, the topics to include in such a workshop are defining plagiarism, detecting plagiarism, and preventing plagiarism. The following sample workshop is designed to include these topics plus a few others that we think are important. Since plagiarism tends to be more prevalent in middle and high schools than in elementary schools, this workshop is geared to secondary level educators.

Planning

Just as with copyright issues, you need to educate yourself on the topic of plagiarism before presenting a workshop. The preceding paragraphs provide excellent background information that you may want to orally share in a workshop presentation. Additionally, the Web sites listed at the end of this chapter will be helpful in obtaining current plagiarism information for educators.

During your planning, find out if there is an academic honesty policy in your school or school district. If a policy exists, you will want to include it as part of your workshop. If there is no current policy, consider forming a committee to write one. The committee should include teachers, administrators, students, and parents.

 Length of Time

This workshop can be presented in a 60 to 90 minute period, with individual follow-up activities offered by the media specialist. Although there are many aspects of plagiarism, it is not nearly as complicated as copyright issues. The topic generally holds the attention of secondary level classroom teachers since most of them have experience with student cheating. In fact, many teachers may be frustrated with student cheating on written assignments and will welcome ideas on how to handle these situations.

 Materials and Equipment

Computers with Internet access are necessary for an effective workshop on this topic. If possible, each teacher should have a computer. No more than two participants should be assigned to a computer. Hands-on computer activities will allow classroom teachers to personally view the sites that are being used by students to plagiarize written assignments. Participants will also access the Internet to view sites that will help them educate their students on ways to avoid plagiarism.

 Getting Participants

Plagiarism is an important topic for all educators. Ideally this workshop should be mandatory for all classroom teachers. It is wise to obtain the support of school administrators who can inform teachers of attendance expectations. If an administrator seems reluctant to do so, it may be helpful to share one or two short articles that include statistics on student cheating and methods of prevention. An initial questionnaire will arouse participants' interest in the staff development topic. Invite your participants to the workshop by placing invitations in each mailbox. The invitation found on the CD-ROM can be adapted to your date, place, and presenter. Fold the invitation twice for a card format.

Deciding on Activities

Determine your workshop objectives before deciding what activities to include. We suggest the following objectives, noting that participants will learn how to:

- Verbalize the definition of plagiarism
- Recognize reasons why students plagiarize
- Identify means of detecting instances of plagiarism
- Identify ways to prevent plagiarism
- Identify methods that teach students how to avoid plagiarism

 Preparing the Materials

Check all computer equipment before the beginning of the workshop, including the computer that you will use to present the PowerPoint slides and those that the participants will use to access the Internet. Have back-up materials ready for the Internet exploration activity in case there are difficulties with Internet connections during the workshop. For example, you can cache the home pages from the sites that you plan to explore in the workshop activities by saving them to a floppy disk or to your desktop. You will need the following materials and equipment for the workshop:

- An agenda
- A handout of the PowerPoint presentation
- Computers with access to the Internet for all participants
- A laminated district or school academic honesty policy, if one exists
- A paraphrasing practice sheet
- A handout of selected resources
- A workshop evaluation
- Pens and pencils

You might want to create a bulletin board display on the topic, including student plagiarism statistics, ways to prevent plagiarism, a copy of the school's academic honesty policy, and an invitation to the workshop. This display will create teacher interest in the topic and alert students to the fact that their teachers are being educated on plagiarism and are aware of ways that students obtain papers from the Internet. The bulletin board and its message can prove to be deterrents of student plagiarism in your school.

Conducting the Workshop

Greet teachers at the door and give them an agenda. If you are providing refreshments, invite the participants to enjoy them. Then direct participants to the computers, where you have placed workshop materials. Placing workshop handouts, pens, and pencils in colorful folders with pockets will make it easy for the participants to access items when needed. After everyone has arrived and is seated, welcome the participants and orally share some background information about the prevalence of student plagiarism. Follow the notes in the PowerPoint presentation for all the activities in this workshop. You can gauge the amount of time needed for each group activity by circulating among the participants.

Evaluation

 When you show the slide asking the participants to fill out the evaluation form, direct the teachers to remove the evaluation form from their folders and complete it. Pass a basket or box around the room to collect the evaluations. The evaluation should determine whether the workshop was helpful to the teachers and if they learned strategies to help decrease student plagiarism in their classes. You will also want to ask if the faculty would welcome additional workshops to explore anti-plagiarism software or examine online anti-plagiarism tutorials.

Follow-Up Activities

One of the most useful ways to follow up this workshop is to provide one-on-one assistance to teachers who would like to work collaboratively with you to design or redesign lesson plans that discourage student plagiarism. If some teachers meet with you and then implement these redesigned assignments in their classrooms, encourage them to share their experiences at a faculty meeting.

 Final Tips

✓ The topic of student plagiarism can be depressing and frustrating for teachers so try to take a positive approach in your workshop.

✓ Encourage your teachers to talk to one another about plagiarism and to discuss it with their students.

✓ Suggest that the school consider having students sign academic honesty policies that contain statements relating to digital cheating.

✓ Be proactive in offering to help teachers design creative assignments that minimize plagiarism opportunities.

✓ Solicit the support of parents in discouraging student plagiarism.

References

American Association of School Librarians & Association for Educational Communications and Technology. (1998). *Information power: Building partnerships for learning*. Chicago: American Library Association.

Brandt, D. Scott. (2002). Copyright's (not so) little cousin, plagiarism. *Computers in Libraries, 22* (5), 39-41.

Bushweller, Kevin. (1999, March). Digital deception: The Internet makes cheating easier than ever. *Electronic School*, 1-8. Retrieved May 27, 2003, from <http://www.electronicschool.com/199903/0399f2.html>

Cummings, Kate. (2003, March). Pushing against plagiarism through creative assignments. *Library Media Connection*, 22-23.

Harris, Robert. (2002). *Anti-plagiarism strategies for research papers*. Retrieved June 8, 2003, from <http://www.virtualsalt.com/antiplag.htm>

Kleiner, Carolyn & Lord, Mary. (1999, Nov. 22). The cheating game: "Everyone's doing it" from grade school to graduate school. *U.S. News & World Report, 127* (20), 55-66.

McKenzie, Jamie. (1998, May). The new plagiarism: Seven antidotes to prevent highway robbery in an electronic age. *From Now On The Educational Technology Journal, 7* (8), 1-11. Retrieved May 28, 2003, from <http://www.fno.org/may98/cov98may.html>

Sorokin, Ellen. (2002, April 10). Poll conducted nationwide finds high schoolers cheating. *The Washington Times*, p. A03.

Selected Resources

Citations

The following are a few sites that provide examples of how to cite materials in several style formats.

Columbia University Press. (2002). *Basic CGOS style*. Retrieved June 11, 2003, from <http://www.Columbia.edu/cu/cup/cgos/idx_basic.html>

Ohio State University Libraries. (2003). *Citation and style guides*. Retrieved June 11, 2003, from <http://www.lib.ohio-state.edu/refweb/resources/style.htm>

University of Arizona Library. (2003). *Citation guide*. Retrieved November 14, 2003, from <http://dizzy.library.arizona.edu/library/type1/tips/data/citation.html>

Detection

These sites provide information about software programs or services to detect plagiarism in research papers.

Eve2. (n.d.) Retrieved June 11, 2003, from <http://www.canexus.com/eve/index.shtml>

RFEIntegriguard. (n.d.). Retrieved June 11, 2003, from <http://rfe.org/Teaching/IntegriGuard.html>

Glatt Plagiarism Services. (n.d.). Retrieved June 11, 2003, from <http://www.plagiarism.com/>

Plagiarism.org. (2003). Retrieved June 11, 2003, from <http://www.plagiarism.org/index.html>

Wordcheck. (2002). Retrieved June 11, 2003, from <http://www.wordchecksystems.com/>

Educating Students

Purdue University Online Writing Lab. (2003). *Avoiding plagiarism*. Retrieved November 14, 2003, from <http://owl.english.purdue.edu/handouts/research/r_plagiar.html>

University of Maine at Farmington Writing Center. (2003). *Synthesis: Using the work of others*. Retrieved November 14, 2003, from <http://www.umf.maine.edu/~library/plagiarism/>

Petrie, M. (2001). *Plagiarism tutorial*. Retrieved November 14, 2003, from <http://yalesecondary.sd34.bc.ca/ tutorials/plagiarism_tutorial.html>

Paper Mills

The following sites provide term papers to users. At some sites the papers are distributed without charge; some give papers away but ask for one in exchange; and others charge fees for papers, generally depending on the length of the paper and whether it is customized work. In addition to accessing these sites, some students also obtain papers through chatrooms or electronic bulletin boards.

ASM Communications. (2000). *A1termpaper*. Retrieved June 11, 2003, from <http://www.a1-termpaper.com/>

Cheater.com. (2003). Retrieved June 11, 2003, from <http://www.cheater.com/>

Cyber essays. (1998). Retrieved June 11, 2003, from <http://www.cyberessays.com/>

Free termpapers international. (2002). Retrieved June 11, 2003, from <http://www.free-term-papers-online.com/freetermpaperonline/startingup.htm>

Genius papers. (n.d.). Retrieved June 11, 2003, from <http://www.geniuspapers.com/>

Loadstone. (2003). *Evil house of cheat*. Retrieved June 11, 2003, from <http://www.cheathouse.com/>

Other people's papers. (2003). Retrieved June 11, 2003, from <http://www.oppapers.com/>

School sucks. (n.d.). Retrieved June 11, 2003, from <http://www.paperstore.net/sahr/>

www.goldenessays.com. (n.d.). Retrieved June 11, 2003, from <http://www.goldenessays.com/>

Prevention

The following sites provide information to teachers and students on ways to prevent plagiarism. Some of the sites have several other links on the same topic.

Center for Excellence in Teaching and Learning. (2001). *Resources for teaching: Plagiarism*. Retrieved June 11, 2003, from <http://www.albany.edu/cetl/resources/pedagogy/plagiarism.html>

Education World. (2002). *Student guide to avoiding plagiarism*. Retrieved June 11, 2001, from <http://www.education-world.com/a_curr/TM/curr390_guide.shtml>

Lee, I. (2002). *A research guide for students*. Retrieved June 11, 2003, from

Open School BC. (2003). *Plagiarism theme page*. Retrieved June 11, 2003, from <http://www.cln.org/themes/plagiarism.html>

University of Alberta Libraries. (2002). *Handouts & online resources for students*. Retrieved June 11, 2003, from <http://www.library.ualberta.ca/guides/plagiarism/handouts/index.cfm>

Writing Tutorial Services, Indiana University. (1998). *Plagiarism: What it is and how to recognize and avoid it*. Retrieved June 11, 2003, from <http://www.Indiana.edu/~wts/wts/plagiarism.html>

 Materials Available on the Accompanying CD-ROM

- Plagiarism Questionnaire
- Invitation
- Agenda
- PowerPoint Presentation
- Paraphrasing Practice Form
- Selected Resources Handout
- Evaluation

Chapter │ 4 │

Going Digital:
Using Digital Cameras
in the Classroom

Background and Information Needs

Digital cameras are among the hottest technology items on the market. Most schools are purchasing digital cameras for administrative, media center, and classroom use. If your school has not already purchased one or more digital cameras, you will want to share with the faculty and administration some of the ways in which the cameras can facilitate administrative responsibilities, improve information literacy skills, and enhance learning.

School-wide uses for digital cameras include:

- Using the photos on school identification cards

- Enhancing school Web sites with images of the school, faculty, and students

- Producing a database of student photos so substitute teachers can easily identify students

- Creating a school yearbook or newspaper, using the digital photos

- Inserting images into public relations brochures or newsletters that are sent home to parents

- Personalizing awards and certificates

- Enhancing and personalizing open house presentations

Digital photos can add to instructional activities, such as:

- Creating bulletin boards or posters that demonstrate how to wash hands properly or to conduct a science project
- Documenting field trips with photos that can be taken and used later in the classroom to stimulate discussion
- Demonstrating a frog dissection in a biology class
- Making multimedia lessons or handouts to illustrate particular points
- Creating a photo journal of the school year

Examples of ways that students can use digital cameras and photos to enhance their assignments include:

- Adding images to essays, such as "What I Did During the Winter Holiday," creating a photo autobiography
- Incorporating digital photos into a report, such as a study of community workers
- Integrating images into an art project to demonstrate the steps that went into creating a final product
- Illustrating a science project

The opportunities for using digital cameras and photos in school settings are nearly limitless. Point out to your teachers that once they learn how to operate a digital camera they will undoubtedly think of many creative, educational ideas for using digital photos in their classrooms.

Your teachers or administrators may question you as to the advantages of purchasing or using digital cameras so you should be prepared to discuss some of the following with them:

- Digital cameras save time because you can shoot photos, transfer them to a computer, edit the images, and even print them in a matter of minutes, rather than waiting for film to be developed.
- Many digital cameras offer a display screen for reviewing once the image is taken, making it easy to decide if you want to retake or delete the photo.
- Beyond the initial investment of purchasing a digital camera, you do not need to buy film or pay for developing. However, it is important to remember that good quality photo paper and color cartridges for computers can be expensive.
- Digital cameras do not require film or chemical processing so they are more environmentally friendly than traditional cameras.
- Electronic images can be quickly and easily transmitted over phone lines to any place in the world.

It is very likely you may be asked to assist in the selection of digital cameras if your school does not already own a camera or is considering replacing or adding to their present camera collections. You should be willing to research the many brands and types of digital cameras. Depending upon the features that you want in a digital camera, prices generally range from around $100 to several thousand dollars. As with many new technologies, the models are often discontinued within a year or two of their release, and newer models with more updated features take their place. Your goal in selecting a camera is to find one that has the necessary features for classroom use. Consider the ease of use, image quality, storage capacity, special features (such as a zoom lens), price, and warranty and support when purchasing (Harmon, 2000). Some of the more expensive models also function as a video camera that records short digital video clips. For most educational purposes you will want to select a camera model that both teachers and students can easily learn to operate.

Digital cameras are designed to record photos on a variety of media, including a floppy diskette, a recordable CD, or a memory card. The digital recorded images can be downloaded from the camera to a computer, and then changed and used in a variety of ways. They can be printed on special photo paper, inserted into computer documents, incorporated into presentations, or posted on a Web site. To change or edit the digital images, you need a graphics editor. Microsoft Windows and MacIntosh operating systems contain simple, basic graphics capabilities. Also, a graphics editor program is often included when you purchase a digital camera.

When selecting a camera, consider its image resolution capability. The resolution of digital images is measured in pixels, which are the number of tiny points of color per square inch. Photos containing more pixels will have better resolution and result in crisper and clearer images. Remember, however, the higher the resolution, the larger your file size will become. Photo images for Web sites need to be at a lower resolution (fewer pixels and smaller file size) so that the Web page can load at an acceptable speed. Minkel (2000) recommends not posting an image on a Web page that is over 50 kilobytes in file size.

For this staff development workshop we have selected the Sony Mavica digital camera, which is widely purchased and used in school settings.

Planning

If you have not had much experience with operating a digital camera, you will need to take many photos and use them in a variety of ways before attempting to conduct staff development for your teachers. Practice by taking some photos in the media center and try inserting them into your media center Web page or making a bulletin board of students and teachers reading their favorite books. When you feel confident about the use of the camera, you can begin to plan staff development for the teachers and administrators. Remember there are several administrative uses for digital cameras, and having a principal support the workshop will most likely increase teacher attendance.

 Length of Time

In your planning you need to decide on the length of this workshop. Take into consideration the time needed to demonstrate the piece of equipment and provide useful hands-on experiences. The number of participants, as well as the number of available volunteer assistants, can influence the length of the program. It is advisable to include some time for refreshments and socialization, particularly if the workshop is conducted at the end of a school day. This workshop will probably take from $1^1/_2$ to 2 hours, depending on the number of participants and how much time you set aside for socialization and refreshments.

Materials and Equipment

In planning for this type of workshop you definitely need to consider the number of cameras available. In order for the workshop participants to see the parts of the camera and have hands-on experiences, there should be no more than four participants for each available camera. If only one camera is available, then consider doing the workshop in small groups or try to borrow cameras from other sources. When demonstrating a piece of equipment, it is important for participants to be able to see the demonstration clearly, have hands-on experiences with the technology, and engage in follow-up opportunities using the equipment. As a result, the number of available cameras and computers will not only affect how you set up your staff development program, but also play a role in how successful the workshop will be in actually getting teachers to follow through with any suggested activities.

If you have several digital cameras that can be used for your presentation, consider soliciting volunteers who will be able to assist teachers in operating the cameras in the workshop. Teachers, students, or media specialists who have had experience with digital cameras (and specifically the one that is being used in the workshop) are candidates for assistants.

 Getting Participants

You should publicize the workshop early and take into consideration the "technophobia" that classroom teachers might have when trying to learn a new technology. Operating a new piece of technology or equipment can be stressful and intimidating for many people, so we recommend creating a flyer or invitation to help alleviate feelings of anxiety. We also suggest you include some ideas on how the teachers can make use of digital cameras. Be specific in the amount of time required as this type of topic requires presence during the entire workshop. You should also request an RSVP for this program if you have a limited number of digital cameras. Having one camera and 30 participants will not result in a successful workshop!

 Deciding on Activities

It's important to identify your workshop objectives before deciding on the activities to include in your staff development. An overall goal for this workshop is to have the participants learn how to operate and use a digital camera to enhance the curriculum. At the end of the staff development program your objectives might include that the participants be able to:

- Identify the parts and controls of a digital camera
- Operate a digital camera
- Save and use images
- Insert an image into a Word document
- Add caption text to a Word document
- Create a bulletin board of photo images
- Identify creative uses for digital camera use in the classroom or other areas of the school

When you decide on specific workshop objectives, you can then plan activities to meet those objectives. Remember to rehearse and time your PowerPoint presentation. It is essential that you are familiar with all parts of the presentation and are competent with the necessary technology.

 Preparing the Materials

Before conducting your workshop you will need the following materials:

- Digital cameras, including the battery chargers (charge the cameras before the session)
- 3.5 inch floppy disks
- Computers with Microsoft Word programs installed
- Electronic "Going Digital" folders on each computer desktop (with the provided Picture Template)
- A color printer, with fresh ink
- A bulletin board with a large "We Went Digital!" sign
- Poster-size easel paper and markers (with an easel or tape for hanging on a wall)
- Handouts of the PowerPoint presentation with three slides per page and lines for taking notes during the presentation
- Handouts of the selected resources

If you are serving refreshments you also need to make the necessary preparations to make the beverages and snacks available at the beginning of the workshop when the teachers are gathering for the workshop.

Conducting the Workshop

Before the participants arrive, have tables set up with no more than four chairs at each table. On each table include an agenda, at least one camera, one floppy disk for each camera, and one handout for each participant. Begin your workshop with a warm welcome and some information from the introductory paragraphs of this chapter. The PowerPoint presentation contains some initial slides for this purpose. You can then continue with the PowerPoint presentation. Be sure to provide all the participants with enough time to locate the parts of the camera and to successfully operate it, but at the same time you need to follow your agenda. In order to be effective, this workshop requires that all the planned activities be completed in the allotted time.

When the teachers are taking photos of each other, circulate throughout the room. If some of the participants are more experienced with digital cameras than others, ask them to assist those who may need help. Remember to praise the efforts of the participants. If some teachers are not happy with the photos they have taken, encourage them to take additional pictures. You might also want to consider commenting on some of the factors that make particularly effective photos (lighting, centering of the subject, etc.).

After all participants have opportunities to take photos of someone else at their table, have them insert the pictures they took into the Word document, using the template that was created in the "Going Digital" folders. They can then add creative or funny captions under the photos. Have them print the photos in color. Instruct the participants to hang their photos on a bulletin board in the media center under a large sign that says "We Went Digital!" If any of the participants would like copies of their photos, suggest that they print extras to take with them.

Before ending the workshop, ask the teachers and administrators (if present) to sit at the tables and brainstorm some ideas for using the digital cameras in their classrooms or in other places throughout the school. One of the PowerPoint slides introduces this activity. Facilitate the exchange by writing participants' ideas on a large sheet of paper placed on an easel or taped to a wall. Encourage teachers to write these shared ideas on their PowerPoint handouts.

Evaluation

 All staff development should include some type of evaluation that relates back to the objectives of the workshop. For this workshop you want to know if the participants were able to successfully use the camera, print photos, and identify ways to use digital camera in the classroom. You may also want to include some evaluation questions that deal with the clarity of your presentation in order to help you improve future staff development sessions.

Follow-Up Activities

It is important that participants practice their skills at operating a digital camera soon after the workshop. During the first few days after the workshop, e-mail the participants and ask if they have taken any photos with the digital cameras. Offer your assistance if they are experiencing any difficulties. Ask all teachers to provide you with a copy of a photo that they have taken in their classroom and mount it on the "We Went Digital!" bulletin board in the media center, under the photo of the teacher who took the picture. You may want to add some construction paper frames for the photos of both the participants and the photos they produced in their classrooms to make a more attractive bulletin board. At your next faculty meeting ask any teachers who are willing to participate to share how they are using a digital camera in their classrooms. When workshop participants are ready to teach their students how to use the digital camera, be prepared to provide assistance, if needed.

There are other staff development sessions that could logically follow this initial workshop. Activities that would help teachers continue their use of digital cameras include:

- Improving photography skills
- Learning how to use a photo editor
- Inserting images into a PowerPoint presentation
- Printing out pictures on photo paper
- Inserting digital images into Web pages

Even if you do not have additional sessions on these topics you should be willing to work with the teachers on a one-to-one basis to acquire the skills mentioned above. You might also set up a display in the media center with handouts on these topics and books dealing with photography or digital cameras.

Final Tips

☑ Provide step-by-step instructions several times to new learners to make them comfortable with the equipment.

☑ Remember to be patient with your participants and provide them with sufficient time to master the camera operations involved in the workshop.

☑ Allow participants to brainstorm ideas for use in their classrooms or school settings to increase the likelihood that they will follow through with the use of digital cameras.

☑ Help participants have fun with this workshop!

References

Harmon, Christy. (2000). Using digital cameras. *Media & Methods, 36* (3), 27.

Minkel, Walter. (2000). Hot shot. *School Library Journal, 46* (7), 42-44.

Selected Resources

Bailey, Steve (2002). *Digital imagery in education: Links to other online resources.* Retrieved November 20, 2002, from <http://www.barstow.k12.ca.us/bhs/faculty/bailey/digital_imagery/web_resources.html>

Boggs, Christie. (2002). *Basic digital camera tutorial.* Retrieved November 19, 2003, from <http://ed.uwyo.edu/Tech/tutorials/digital_cam.htm>

Curtin, Dennis P. (2003). *ShortCourses Publishing Company.* Retrieved November 20, 2002, from <http://www.shortcourses.com/guides/guides.htm>

Dendy, Francis & Pennock, Faustina. (1998). *Using a digital camera in the classroom.* Retrieved November 20, 2002, from <http://geocities.com/Athens/Olympus/7123/camera.html>

Eastman Kodak Company. (2002). *Digital learning center plus: Chapter V teachers/ leaders.* Retrieved November 21, 2002, from <http://www.kodak.com/US/en/digital/dlc/plus/chapter5/indexs.html>

How to use the Sony Mavica digital camera.(n.d.). Retrieved November 20, 2002, from <http://scnc.perry.k12.mi.us/Mavica.html>

Judd, Diane (n.d.). *"How to" take pictures with a digital camera.* Retrieved November 20, 2002, from <http://www.valdosta.edu/~djudd/camera.html>

Lycos. (2002). *Digital cameras.* Retrieved November 20, 2002, from <http://howto.lycos.com/lycos/topic/0,,26041,00.html>

Plano, ISD. (2000). *Digital camera resources.* Retrieved November 20, 2002, from
<http://k-12.pisd.edu/multimedia/camera.htm>

Vieira, Mary (2002). *Sony Mavica digital cameras.* Retrieved November 20, 2002, from
<http://enrollmentoptions.sandi.net/workshops/digitalimages/mavicaiphoto.html>

 Materials Available on the Accompanying CD-ROM

- Flyer
- Agenda
- PowerPoint Presentation

- Picture Template
- Resources Handout
- Evaluation

* Photo images of the SONY FD Mavica used on the accompanying CD are "Courtesy of Sony Electronics Inc."

Chapter 5

Chapter 5

Joining the Web:

Designing Classroom

Web Pages

Background and Information Needs

People are going online to obtain assistance in numerous areas of their lives—shopping for products, paying their bills, filling out tax returns, communicating with friends and professionals, obtaining health information, planning travel, and being entertained. The provision of online information from educational settings has also become commonplace. As parents and students become more proficient with the use of the Internet in their daily lives, they are expecting schools to provide online information. Thus, school and classroom Web sites have become a popular means of keeping parents and students up to date on what is happening in their schools. Schools sometimes call upon a "techie" at the school or district level to design a school Web site, but we are seeing more and more schools provide Web pages for individual classrooms and teachers, in addition to the official school site. These Web pages are a new mode of communication, as well as a way to feature student work done in the classrooms. Consequently, it is important that classroom teachers learn how to design and maintain their individual classroom sites.

Why Design a Classroom Web Page?

A classroom Web page is an efficient means of communicating with students, parents, and the community to keep them informed about what is happening in a classroom. The type of news that usually goes home in a newsletter to parents can be posted on the Web page. Information about discipline, classroom procedures, homework assignments, and grading policies can be shared with both students and parents. Students at all levels enjoy accessing information online and are usually eager to utilize (and help produce) a classroom Web page. However, teachers may need to get parents used to the idea of regularly checking a classroom site. This can be done by posting an announcement and a link on the school's main Web page, providing the URL and a demonstration at a school's open house, and/or sending home a notice to parents informing them of the classroom Web page. Making take-home magnets with the name of the site and URL and suggesting that the magnets be placed on the refrigerators in their homes is another way of publicizing the use of the site. Once parents realize that they can keep up with their children's education through such means, they will find their efforts are rewarding.

When teachers involve students in the creation of a classroom Web page, it becomes an excellent learning experience. Students can acquire technology skills, such as keyboarding, desktop publishing, and conversion of files and graphics. They can learn how to locate, gather, and evaluate Internet resource sites. They will be challenged to use their creativity in designing a Web page and can learn some of the elements of good Web design. Involving students also gives them a sense of belonging, practice in cooperative learning activities, and motivation to utilize the classroom Web site (Charland, 1998).

What Should a Classroom Web Page Include?

Teachers can make their classroom pages as simple or as involved as they choose. However, if the site is a teacher's initial attempt at creating a Web page, it is a good idea to keep the design and types of information fairly basic. The most important aspect of creating a Web page is to define one's goals—what is it that the teacher wishes to accomplish through the Web site? The teacher should consider who will be visiting the Web site and what kind of information will be provided to them (Warlick, 2002). The following are some of the most frequent types of information offered on classroom Web pages:

- The teacher's instructional objectives and expectations
- Classroom news and announcements, such as an upcoming field trip
- Homework assignments
- A classroom calendar of events and/or topics of study for a semester
- Showcasing of student work

  Other types of helpful information include:

- Links to sites that help students find information for assignments or research projects
- Links to tutorials or practice exercises that can assist students with specific educational skills
- Links to parenting resources

- Links to community resources, such as libraries, historical societies, or museums
- A means of contacting the teacher through e-mail (although this can be an efficient way of communicating with parents and students, some teachers may find the volume of such e-mail can be overwhelming)
- A discussion board

Some school districts have policies on Web page content; therefore, it is a good idea to check to see if such a policy exists in your district. It is important to protect the safety of students and their identities when creating a Web page. Also, all copyright laws should be adhered to and the content and appearance of the page should follow professional standards (Peto & McGlone, 1998).

Where Can Teachers Get Help in Designing Web Pages?

You don't need to be a "techie" to create a Web page, nor do you need to know HTML (Hypertext Mark-Up Language), although a basic knowledge of HTML is helpful in creating and maintaining a Web site. Fortunately, there are many software programs and online Web building tools. Some of the most popular programs like Microsoft's FrontPage, Macromedia's Dreamweaver, Hyperstudios's SiteCentral, and Netscape Composer are relatively easy to use.

There are also several Internet sites that offer access to free software to create Web pages and free Web site space. Some of these sites are available only to certain types of users, such as small businesses or schools, while others are open to anyone. Most of the sites have templates that are used to reduce the work involved in creating a Web page. Some sites place advertising on their sites as well as on the created Web pages, while others place restrictions on the format of pages; consequently, it is advisable to read all conditions that accompany a Web page building service (Clyde, 2001).

The following are some sites that provide free Web page construction and Web site hosting space for schools:

- Class Homepage Builder <http://teacher.scholastic.com/homepagebuilder/index.htm>
- Classroom.tripod.com <http://classroom.tripod.com />
- Myschoolonline.com <http://www.myschoolonline.com>
- School Center <http://schoolcenter.com>
- TeacherWeb.com <http://teacherweb.com>
- Teachers.net <http://www.teachers.net>

Helpful Tips for Building a Web Page

As mentioned previously, beginning Web designers will probably want to make their Web pages relatively simple and not include several pages on one site. The following tips will help teachers build effective Web pages:

- Include only information that you think will be helpful to your audience and that meets the objectives of your Web page.
- The front page should be welcoming and should load quickly.
- Do not include a lot of graphics since this will lengthen the time to access the site; however, a few well-chosen graphics can be very effective.

- If you want photos on your Web page, use a digital camera to eliminate the need to scan photos.
- Do not place photos of students on the page without written permission from a parent or guardian.
- Student work and photos should be identified only by a first name.
- Be certain navigation on the pages is simple, consistent, and logical. Create a diagram or flowchart when designing the pages to help you plan how users will navigate through the site.
- If creating more than one page for the site, make certain every page has a "return to the home page" link.
- Keep all pages consistent in format. Using a master template will help create pages that are consistent in appearance and navigation.
- Keep scrolling to a minimum.
- Use colors that complement each other and are not overwhelming to users.
- Remember to include white space on the pages. Overuse of space can interfere with the effectiveness of the information presented.
- Keep headings simple and flush left, rather than centered.
- Edit the page thoroughly to make certain grammar, spelling, and punctuation are accurate.
- Test all links periodically to see if they are working.
- When linking to other sites, link directly to the pages that provide the "good" information. Be certain you are linking only to sites that are developmentally appropriate.
- Include disclaimers whenever personal opinions are expressed so the site visitors understand that the opinions are not necessarily those of the school or school district.
- Have a committee review the site before posting it on a server.
- Link the site to the school's home page.
- Submit the URL to major search engines and directories.

Planning

We have selected Microsoft's Front Page for this teacher workshop. The program is commonly used to build Web pages and is often available in schools. If you have not built a Web page using Microsoft FrontPage, it will be necessary for you to do so. In fact, you should practice making several simple pages so you will be familiar with the various aspects of the program. Generally there is a wide variety of computer knowledge and skills among the teachers in a school so it would be wise to determine the skill level of the participants before conducting this workshop. You may want to divide the faculty into groups according to their computer skills and conduct more than one workshop. If all the classroom teachers are grouped together, it may be difficult to pace the workshop activities. However, if you do decide to include all teachers in the same staff development workshop, be sure to have some assistants available to help participants who experience difficulties while developing their Web pages. Also, it is an excellent idea to conduct this workshop collaboratively with any technology personnel at your school.

 Length of Time

The length of time for this workshop will depend on the complexity of the Web pages that participants create, as well as their computer skills. Providing some background information and having teachers each build a simple classroom Web page will probably take at least 90 minutes.

 Materials and Equipment

Your goal is for each teacher to build a classroom Web page. Thus, it is essential that each participant have access to a computer. Additionally, you will need to have Microsoft Front Page software with a license for the number of participants who will be using the program during the workshop. If your school license has a limit on the number of users, this would be another reason to offer this workshop with smaller groups of teachers.

 Getting Participants

Some teachers will be intimidated by the concept of building a classroom Web page so you should try to advertise this workshop by emphasizing that step-by-step procedures will be provided. You should also let the teachers know how a classroom Web page can be helpful to them, their students, and parents. It is probably not a good idea to make this workshop mandatory. It is better for some teachers to experience success in the workshop and then let "word of mouth" advertise for any future workshops you offer on the topic. Participants need to be committed to the idea of both building and maintaining a classroom Web page, since it is a time-consuming endeavor.

 Deciding on Activities

Determine the objectives of your staff development workshop before you decide which activities to include. In our workshop we plan to share the benefits of having a classroom Web page with the participants, and then have each teacher make a basic Web page using Microsoft FrontPage. Additionally, we want to inform the participants about some of the free Web sites they can access to build Web pages, and encourage them to involve their students in making a classroom Web page. Thus, our objectives are:

- Identify the purposes of a classroom Web page.
- Discuss the benefits of involving students in the creation and maintenance of a classroom Web page.
- Consider helpful tips in building a Web page.
- Identify other tools for building Web pages.
- Build a basic Web page.
- Discuss the follow-up procedures of the workshop.

Although some introduction to the staff development topic is important, remember to reserve plenty of time for the participants to build a classroom Web page. For this workshop to be successful, each participant should be able to walk out the door with a simple working Web page that can be posted to a server. If participants wish to build more into their pages, this can be done in follow-up activities. The PowerPoint presentation at the end of the chapter and on the CD-ROM that accompanies this book relates the activities that can be used to fulfill the stated objectives.

 Preparing the Materials

Materials needed to conduct this workshop are:

- An agenda
- Computers with Microsoft's FrontPage loaded onto each computer
- 3.5 inch floppy disks for each participant if server storage space is not available
- A handout of the PowerPoint presentation with three slides per page and lines for taking notes during the workshop
- Pens or pencils
- A handout of the Directions Sheet
- A handout of Selected Resources
- A workshop evaluation
- A certificate of completion

Conducting the Workshop

Before the teachers arrive for the workshop check all the computers to make certain they are in working order. Also, load your PowerPoint presentation and do a quick run-through to remind you of the workshop procedures. Place a PowerPoint handout at each computer desk, along with a pen or pencil that can be used to take notes.

Welcome the teachers and begin the workshop by showing the participants some examples of classroom Web pages. We have listed some at the end of this chapter that can be used for this purpose or you can select some. If there are teachers in the local school districts with Web pages, be sure to include some of those sites. Show a few good examples of sites, including some basic, but well-designed sites. After you have demonstrated a few sites, move right into the PowerPoint presentation in which you will conduct activities that meet the objectives of the workshop. Don't progress too rapidly through the steps involved with building the Web pages. You do not want participants to get behind or lost in the process. Move about the room or have volunteer assistants walk among the participants and help as needed.

Before ending the workshop talk about some of the follow-up activities that may need to take place before posting the Web pages to a server: reviewing and editing the content, checking to make certain all the content meets copyright guidelines, and asking for student input and possible involvement.

At the end of the workshop present each participant with a certificate of accomplishment for gaining the skills to build a classroom Web page.

Evaluation

 You should include some questions on the evaluation that deal with the clarity, content, and usefulness of the workshop. You should also ask participants if they are interested in additional workshops to add to or improve their Web pages. Provide a place where the participants can deposit their anonymous evaluation forms.

Follow-Up Activities

It is important to follow up this workshop by offering some one-on-one assistance to each classroom teacher so their Web pages can be posted to a server and function for their classrooms. A few days after the workshop e-mail the teachers thanking them for their attendance. Ask them to set up a time to meet with you or the technology teacher to complete any steps that need to be taken before placing the pages on a server. If some teachers do not respond, try again a few days later and tell the teachers that you are looking forward to seeing their classroom Web pages on the server.

If enough teachers have expressed interest on your evaluation form, consider setting up an additional workshop to add to the teachers' Web pages. Before conducting such a workshop, allow several weeks for the teachers, students and parents to utilize their classroom Web pages. Then suggest that they jot down ideas for improvements or additions to their pages. Encourage them to get student and parent input as well. If any teachers want to involve students in the design and improvement of their Web pages, consider inviting some of the students to accompany their teacher to an additional workshop.

Remember to send thank you notes and perhaps provide a small gift to those who assisted you with this workshop.

When all workshop participants have posted their classroom Web pages to a server, ask permission at an upcoming faculty meeting to briefly showcase the pages. Hopefully, this will encourage reluctant teachers to consider building Web pages for their classrooms.

Final Tips

☑ Keep things simple without including bells and whistles on the participants' Web pages.

☑ Stick to the time limitations; don't get side-tracked.

☑ Remember that Web pages created in FrontPage may look different when viewed in Internet Explorer and Netscape.

☑ Take advantage of the online help, articles, and books on this topic.

☑ Encourage participants to further develop their Web pages and to make them unique (perhaps at another workshop).

Materials Available on the Accompanying CD-ROM

- Flyer
- Agenda
- PowerPoint Presentation
- Web Directions Sheet

- Sample Classroom Web Page
- Resources Handout
- Evaluation
- Certificate

References

Charland, Tammy S. (1998). Classroom homepage connections; Technological horizons in education. *T.H.E. Journal, 25* (9), 62-64.

Clyde, Anne. (2001). Free web site hosting. *Teacher Librarian, 29* (1), 49-50.

Peto, Erica & McGlone, Ann. (1998). *School home page building blocks*. Retrieved June 16, 2003, from <http://www.learningspace.org/content/default.html>

Warlick, David. (2002, September). Plan it. Design it. Build it. Put your Web site to work. *Technology & Learning, 23* (2), 22-31.

Selected Resources

Books

Hixson, Susan & Schrock, Kathleen. (1998). *Developing Web pages for school and classroom*. Westminster, California: Teacher Created Materials.

Holden, Greg. (1997). *Creating Web pages for kids & parents*. Chicago: IDG Books Worldwide.

Logan, Debra K. & Beuselinck, Cynthia. (2001). *K-12 Web pages: Planning and publishing excellent school Web sites*. Worthington, Ohio: Linworth Publishing Co.

Wigglebits, Wanda. (2002). *Building a school Web site: A hands-on project for teachers and kids*. Chicago: Duomo Press.

Web Sites

Bellingham Public Schools. (2003). *Design tenets for web pages*. Retrieved June 13, 2003, from <http://www.bham.wednet.edu/technology/webtenets.htm>

Burns, Joe. (2003). *Basic HTML.Primer #1:Introduction/what you will need*. Retrieved June 12, 2003, from <http://www.htmlgoodies.com/primers/primer_1.html>

McKenzie, Jamie. (2003). *Designing school Web sites to deliver*. Retrieved June 12, 2003, from <http://www.fno.org/webdesign.html>

Peto, Erica & McGlone, Ann. (1998). *School home page building blocks*. Retrieved June 16, 2003, from <http://www.learningspace.org/content/default.html>

Plano Independent School District. (2002). *Plano ISD school Web page guidelines*. Retrieved June 16, 2003, from <http://k-12.pisd.edu/guide/schools/webpages>

Schrock, Kathleen. (2003). *About the Internet, HTML, and graphics*. Retrieved June 16, 2003, from <http://school.discovery.com/schrockguide/yp/iyabout.html>

Chapter 6

Inspector Quest:

Designing Inquiry-Based

Web Projects

Background and Information Needs

In recent years many schools have adopted an inquiry-based approach to learning. This instructional approach involves students using quests to find answers to their questions and sharing their findings. In inquiry-based learning classrooms, students learn by building on their own understanding of experiences. They are encouraged to help construct questions and are provided with opportunities to solve problems.

The constructivist theory of learning serves as the foundation for inquiry-based learning. In this theory, learning is viewed as an active process in which the learner is continually constructing knowledge that has meaning to that particular learner (Kuhlthau, 2001). Students not only find the answers to their questions, but they also spend time reflecting on what they have learned and trying to make sense of it. This type of learning engages students in higher order thinking skills, rather than shallow responses to superficial questions, which may have little meaning to the learner.

Inquiry-based learning centers on the research process, a process in which students identify problems or questions. Students are guided in the research process of locating, evaluating, and interpreting information related to their questions. Then they apply the information and transform it by using it in new ways that have meaning to the students.

Teachers who want to engage students in inquiry-based learning in their classrooms should use instructional lessons that emanate naturally from their curriculum. They need to develop questions based on curriculum standards that will help initiate the inquiry process. Resources for answering these questions should be readily available to students. Since students learn in many different ways, a variety of resource formats are essential to accommodate students' individual needs.

How Can Internet Resources Be Used to Enhance Inquiry-Based Learning?

There are several types of Internet quests that utilize inquiry-based learning approaches. Scavenger hunts, Internet treasure hunts, guided tour assignments, and WebQuests are some of the terms that describe structured assignments that use Web resources to guide students to explore ideas, answer questions, and solve problems. All of these lesson designs help educators integrate the use of technology, specifically the Internet, into classrooms.

San Diego State University professors, Bernie Dodge and Tom March, introduced the term *WebQuest* in 1995 when they devised a model to integrate the World Wide Web into the classroom (Lipscomb, 1998). Dodge (1995) describes a WebQuest as "an inquiry-oriented activity in which some or all of the information that learners interact with comes from resources on the internet, optionally supplemented with videoconferencing." The concept of WebQuests has become extremely popular with educators, and literally hundreds of WebQuests have been posted to the World Wide Web. In many instances these lessons have been submitted directly to Dodge, who maintains a Web site with sample WebQuests. Many teachers simply utilize these already developed quest projects. Other teachers adapt the projects for use in their classrooms, while some teachers take on the task of learning how to develop inquiry-based Web projects that meet the needs of their students and their curriculum standards.

Assistance is available for educators who want to learn how to develop inquiry-based activities that use the Internet. Much of this help can be found on the Web itself. WebQuest templates and other interactive Web sites, such as *Filamentality* (www.kn.pacbell.com/wired/fil) guide teachers through the process of selecting questions, searching the Web for good information that relates to the questions, and developing learning activities that use the Web resources. There are also online tutorials that help teachers learn to develop their own quests, as well as rubrics that can be used to help educators and students evaluate the inquiry-based assignments.

One of the benefits of using structured lessons that involve Internet resources is that it saves students' time by allowing them to concentrate on evaluating and using information, rather than spending huge amounts of time "surfing the Net" for information. Other benefits include obtaining cooperative learning skills, since most inquiry-based Web projects require that students cooperatively answer questions that relate to the real world. For some projects, students select specific roles and responsibilities that are outlined in the assignments, thus enabling students to take advantage of their various strengths and interests. The project tasks frequently require students to use other technology skills, such as e-mail, databases, or spreadsheets. In sharing the information they have learned, students are sometimes motivated to create videos or multimedia projects. The various skills that students learn in these research processes go far beyond fact-based learning; they provide the tools that will help students to continue learning independently long after they are out of school (Murray, 2003).

What Are the Basic Components of an Inquiry-Based Web Project?

An inquiry-based Web project consists of several components. The names of these parts, or steps, may vary in different models, but they generally consist of the following:

- **The Introduction.** The introduction should capture the attention of the students by presenting relevant questions or an authentic problem that they are being asked to solve. Ideally, students can have some input into this section of the project since inquiry-based learning should emanate from questions raised by the students. Questions should relate to the curriculum, but they do not have to be limited to one discipline. In fact, many inquiry-based projects are interdisciplinary. It is recommended that the questions or problems build on the previous learning of students. The teacher may want to provide some additional background information on the problem in this introductory section.

- **The Task.** This section should clearly state the tasks that the students are to accomplish. If the project includes a real-life scenario, the teacher may want to describe roles that students are to assume in order to complete the project. Some of the roles can be similar in nature, encouraging student collaboration and sharing.

- **The Sources of Information.** In this section the teacher should provide the students with the resources they will use to complete their tasks. Web sites that have been carefully selected by the teacher and media specialist should be listed. Other sources, such as searchable databases and experts who are available by e-mail, can also be included. If the teacher wishes to have the students utilize print sources available in the media center, these can be a part of the listing. It is helpful to group Web sites with similar types of information or have brief annotations of the sources so students can determine which sources might be most helpful to them.

- **The Process.** This section should include the steps that the teacher wants the students to follow to complete the task.

- **The Product.** In this section provide students with guidance about the format of the products they will develop to share their findings. If the students have a choice of products, those choices should be listed.

- **Evaluation.** Both self-evaluation and teacher evaluation are encouraged in inquiry-based learning. Rubrics developed by the teacher (perhaps with student input) can be used for evaluation purposes and should be available to the students so they are aware of the criteria that will be used to grade their efforts. The evaluations should include items relating to the research process, the product, and collaborative efforts.

Inquiry-based Web projects can be fairly simple in nature, requiring only two or three class sessions to complete or they can be much more complex, as with a scenario. These latter projects may take several days or even weeks to complete.

How Can Media Specialists Assist with Inquiry-Based Web Projects?

Developing inquiry-based Web projects are ideal opportunities for collaboration between school media specialists and teachers. School media specialists can assist teachers in the selection of a research model that will guide students in their quests. They also should make certain that teachers are aware of the nine information literacy standards presented in the American Association of School Librarians national guidelines and integrate these skills into the inquiry-based Web projects. The actual development of the project can be a cooperative effort in which the teacher informs the media specialist which curriculum standards are being addressed in the project. The media specialist assists in the development of meaningful, relevant questions or problems, as well as in locating quality Web sites and other resources that students can use to answer the project questions or solve the problems.

School media specialists can also present a staff development workshop that introduces teachers to the benefits of inquiry-based projects and provides step-by-step guidance on developing projects for their classroom settings. The following paragraphs describe such a workshop.

Planning

Make certain that you are familiar with the philosophy of inquiry-based learning before conducting this workshop. A quick, but efficient, method of doing this, besides reviewing the introductory paragraphs of this chapter, is to read the first chapter of *Inquiry-Based Learning: Lessons from Library Power* (Linworth, 2001). Since you want teachers to collaborate in developing the inquiry-based Web projects, it is probably best if teachers from similar areas of the curriculum or the same grade levels attend the workshop together. The participants may require a fair amount of your time as the groups develop separate projects, so consider limiting the number of workshop attendees to approximately 9 to 12 people. In your initial invitation or flyer ask the participants to come to the workshop with ideas for assignments that could include the use of Web resources.

 Length of Time

This workshop involves some hands-on tasks by the participants. If the major portions of their projects are designed during the workshop, the teachers will be more likely to follow through and complete their projects and use them with their students. The workshop requires approximately two hours.

 Materials and Equipment

At least one computer with Internet access should be available for each small group of participants (3 to 4 in a group). If possible, having a computer for each participant is advised since this will make it possible for participants to divide up some of the tasks involved in designing their projects.

 Getting Participants

You may want to attend departmental or grade level meetings to introduce the idea for this workshop. If possible, try to obtain the support of the department chair or lead person in the grade level before attending a meeting. It would also be helpful to gain administrative support from the principal or curriculum coordinator. At the meeting, briefly explain the idea of inquiry-based learning and demonstrate a couple of the interesting WebQuests or scavenger hunts that can be found online. Be sure to select quests that correlate with the teachers' subject areas or that are appropriate for their grade levels. Consider sharing a simple quest and then a more complex quest where a scenario is presented and roles are assigned.

 Deciding on Activities

In order to help us decide what activities to include in this workshop, we developed the following objectives:

- Define inquiry-based learning and inquiry-based Web projects.
- Identify benefits of inquiry-based Web projects.
- Demonstrate the development of an inquiry-based Web project.
- Develop inquiry-based Web projects.

For this topic it is essential that participants understand the philosophy of inquiry-based learning, as well as the benefits to the students. Thus, it is important to begin this workshop with these two concepts.

As mentioned previously, inquiry-based Web projects can be fairly simple and straightforward and involve only a few class periods or they can be complex and require several days or weeks for the students to complete. Due to time limitations for our workshop, we decided to demonstrate a simple project, without a scenario. Participants in the workshop will be given the opportunity to design either simple or more complex tasks.

 Preparing the Materials

You will need to prepare the following materials before you conduct the workshop and make them available to participants:

- An agenda
- A handout of the PowerPoint presentation, with three slides per page and space for the participants to take notes
- A 3.5 inch floppy disk for each participant or group of participants (depending on the number of available computers) containing a template for designing the Web project
- A handout of selected resources
- An evaluation form

In addition, before the workshop begins you should check your equipment to make certain all the computers are in working order and Internet access is available. You will also want a copy of the Inquiry-Based Web Project Workshop Topic Sheet available.

Conducting the Workshop

If possible, provide some refreshments at the beginning of the workshop and keep them available for participants during the time that they design their Web projects since this workshop will most likely be fairly long. Remind the participants to keep all food and drinks away from the computers. Having some empty tables with chairs will facilitate this.

After participants have had an opportunity to enjoy refreshments, ask them to gather at the computers with teachers from their own grade level or subject areas. Welcome the participants and immediately begin the PowerPoint presentation, using the notes provided for each slide.

During the time that the participants are designing their inquiry-based Web projects, be sure to circulate among the groups and assist them in finding good Web sites, bookmarking those sites, saving the bookmarks to floppy disks, and filling in the templates on the disks. Remember to encourage the participants and praise them for their efforts.

Evaluation

Evaluation for this workshop should focus not only on the clarity of your presentation, but whether the participants have learned enough to successfully design and utilize an inquiry-based Web project with their students.

Follow-Up Activities

It is especially important that the media specialist be available for follow-up for this workshop. You will have a list of the groups' topics, grade levels or subject areas, and participants' names on your Inquiry-Based Web Project Workshop Topic Sheet. Be sure to contact the teachers who participated in the workshop and provide your assistance for the design and implementation of the projects. Ask them when they plan to meet again to work on their projects, if they are not already completed. Attend those meetings, if possible.

Most likely the implementation of many of the projects will utilize the computers in the media center, so you may want to bookmark the resources for the students when they come to the media centers to complete their projects.

Let the teachers know that you are available to assist in any other Web projects they want to design. Encourage collaboration from the planning stage through implementation and evaluation.

Final Tips

☑ Find some creative and interesting quests online to share with the teachers at an initial meeting since you will want to get them excited about designing their own inquiry-based Web projects.

☑ Offer to have final products from the Web projects displayed in the media center, along with a copy of the design of the project.

☑ When teachers have become proficient at designing Web-based projects, encourage them to teach the process to their students.

☑ Keep abreast of current topics of interest in a variety of subjects and make a file of topics so you can be ready to present possible ideas to teachers for inquiry-based Web projects. Solicit ideas from students for your file.

References

Dodge, Bernie. (1997). *Some thoughts about WebQuests*. Retrieved August 3, 2003, from <http://edweb.sdsu.edu/courses/edtec596/about_webquests.html>

Kuhlthau, Carol Collier. (2001). Inquiry-based learning. In Jean Donham, Kay Bishop, Carol Collier Kuhlthau, and Dianne Oberg, (Authors), *Inquiry-based learning: Lessons from Library Power* (pp. 1-12). Worthington, OH: Linworth.

Lipscomb, George. (2003, January/February). "I guess it was pretty fun": Using WebQuests in the middle school classroom. *The Clearing House*. Retrieved June 23, 2003, from ProQuest database.

Murray, Janet. (2003, March/April). Contemporary literacy: Essential skills for the 21st century. *Multimedia Schools*. Retrieved June 23, 2003, from ProQuest database.

Selected Resources

Articles

Brooks-Young, Susan; MacKay, Pete & Solomon, Gwen. (2003). Building and using WebQuests. *Technology & Learning, 23* (6), 32-33.

Junion-Metz, Gail. (2002). World Wide WebQuests. *School Library Journal, 48* (7), 29.

Peterson, Cynthia; Caverly, David C. & MacDonald, Lucy. (2003). Techtalk: Developing academic literacy through WebQuests. *Journal of Developmental Education, 26* (3), 152-155.

Salpeter, Judy. (2003). Web literacy and critical thinking. A teacher's tool kit. *Technology & Learning, 23* (8), 22-29.

Van Leer, Jerilyn. (2003). Teaching information and technology literacy through student-created WebQuests. *Multimedia Schools, 10* (2), 42-45.

Watson, Kenneth Lee. (1999). WebQuests in the middle school curriculum: Promoting technological literacy in the classroom. *Meridian: A Middle School Computer Technologies Journal, 2* (2). Retrieved November 11, 2003, from <http://www.ncsu.edu/meridian/jul99/webquest/index.html>

Web Sites

Dodge, Bernie. (2003). *TheWebQuest page.* Retrieved November 11, 2003, from <http://www.webquest.sdsu.edu/webquest.html>

Gurian, Linda. (2000). *The elementary Webquest?ion: A WebQuest about WebQuests for 1st through 5th grade teachers.* Retrieved November 11, 2003, from <http://www.teachtheteachers.org/projects/LGurian3/top.htm>

Ruffini, Michael F. (2002). *WebQuest knowledge map.* Retrieved November 11, 2033, from <http://www.mapacourse.com/webquest%20html/webquest%20icon.html>

Schrock, Kathleen. (2003). *Web quest in our future: The teacher's role in Cyberspace.* Retrieved June 23, 2003, from <http://school.discovery.com/schrockguide/webquest/webquest.html>

Focused on the future. Spartanburg School District 3. Retrieved November 11, 2003, from <http://www.spa3.k12.sc.us/WebQuests.html>

 Materials Available on the Accompanying CD-ROM

- Flyer
- Agenda
- PowerPoint Presentation: Designing Inquiry-Based Web Projects
- Project Template

  This will need to be dowloaded onto each floppy disk used by the participants. The participants can fill in the template with their specific information.

- Media Specialist's Web Project Topic Sheet
- Evaluation Form

Chapter ⎡7⎤

Pennywise: Conducting Virtual Field Trips

Background and Information Needs

The Internet has opened new kinds of adventures in connecting subject content to the curriculum. One of the most interesting areas for students and teachers has been the use of online field trips. These virtual field trips are online versions of traditional field trips, which research has long demonstrated as having educational value for students. Field trips add variety to instruction, while at the same time they motivate students and provide them with relevant, meaningful learning that can be utilized outside the classroom setting. Field trips are often made to locations such as museums, zoos, aquariums, or outdoor settings. Unfortunately, with tight education budgets and other problems associated with traditional field trips, many schools are not providing these types of experiences for their students. The authors of this book believe that actual field trips have much value to students and should not be abandoned. However, in this chapter we will present alternatives to the traditional school field trips.

What Are Virtual Field Trips?

Stevenson (2001) defines virtual field trips as "computergenerated [sic] environments that offer media-rich interactions with a particular location, such as laboratories, museums, parks, zoos, and even other countries" (p. 43). They are often free, but sometimes fees are involved, particularly if multiple trips are required.

Although they may seem somewhat similar, virtual field trips and online expeditions are two different forms of technology-enriched curriculum support. Virtual field trips usually make it possible for students to explore a particular destination and are generally designed for a one-time visit (Ashton, 2002). Online expeditions, however, are normally educational experiences where students are exploring places and things in real time. Often the expeditions are interactive and students are able to ask questions, listen to the actual persons carrying out the expeditions, and perhaps chat with other students who are also viewing the expedition online. An example of such an expedition is *The Jason Project* (<http:// www.Jason project.org/>), which allows students from across the country to listen to scientists carry out underwater expeditions, visit volcanoes and rain forests, and participate in a variety of other interesting scientific expeditions around the world. *NOAA's aquarius*: *America's Interspace Station* (<http://www.uncwil.edu/nurc/aquarius/>) makes it possible for participants to come aboard a ten-day underwater laboratory mission in the Florida Keys. Some of the expeditions are free, while others, such as the Jason Project, are fee-based.

In this chapter we focus on online virtual field trips, rather than expeditions; however, many of the suggestions made for this workshop could be applied to online expeditions.

How Can Virtual Field Trips Be Incorporated into the Curriculum?

The most important reason for having a virtual field trip is to connect the content of the field trip to the curriculum. This should always be the primary goal of a virtual field trip. Teachers can meet this goal by reviewing school, state or national standards in their disciplines. Additionally, through online field trips, the students will meet some of the National Educational Technology Standards for Students (available at <http://cnets.iste.org/students/s_stands.html>), such as developing positive attitudes toward technology, using technology to enhance learning, and becoming proficient in the use of technology (Wilton & Foley, 2003).

There are some specific ways that a virtual field trip can be incorporated into the curriculum. If a class is going to take an actual field trip, the teacher can do an all-class preview of the site, using a projection screen, or students can individually access the online resources to introduce them to what they will see on the trip. Previewing the site in this way can sensitize students to stimuli they will encounter at the actual site and help them focus on relevant and required tasks when they take the actual trip. The Web-based tours can also lay an informational foundation and encourage students to prepare questions for further investigation. Being familiar with the layout and logistics of the destination can also assist teachers in planning agendas of the actual trips (times of operation, entrances, location of restrooms, etc.). Some sites provide discount coupons or free passes for educators, so it can be economically advantageous to access a site before the actual field trip (Cox-Petersen & Melber, 2001). Many sites also provide specific information for visiting school groups.

Another way to use a virtual field trip is in the follow-up activities of an actual field trip. Students may have some questions that can be answered by accessing the online tour or a teacher might want to use the virtual field trip to stimulate further discussion and reinforce learning from the actual field trip. Additionally, some sites have interactive games or streaming videos that can help students learn more about a particular topic. Teachers can also make comparisons between a virtual field trip and an actual trip to the identical location to determine which type of trip is most beneficial.

Most teachers use virtual field trips when an actual visit is not possible. There are, of course, some disadvantages of virtual field trips since they generally tend to be more passive and the students are unable to interact directly with the personnel at selected locations. School computers may not be up to speed on the hardware and software that is required to participate in a virtual field trip; thus, a teacher may have to make certain all computers have the technology requirements. Also, some initial teaching of technology skills might be necessary. If students are being asked to access the field trip from home (and perhaps share the experience with a parent), this will be even more of a problem. One must also consider the fact that not all students will have computers with Internet access at home.

When planning an online virtual field trip, most teachers ask students to visit a single site. However, "threaded" virtual field trips, in which various tour sites have been selected by educators and arranged in "threads" that students can access, make it possible for students to learn about a topic or theme from several sites and experts. *Tramline* (<http://www.field-trips.org/trips.htm>) is an award-winning site that provides these types of virtual field trips.

A final means of utilizing virtual field trips is for teachers to create their own virtual field trips. By utilizing digital cameras, audio and video components, and Web-authoring software, teachers are able to tailor their virtual field trips to the needs of their students and adjust the content to match the actual curriculum (Tuthill & Klemm, 2002). This type of virtual field trip is ideal for local sites that do not have a presence on the Internet. These might include historical sites, parks, schools, or small museums. Some Web pages that provide directions for producing teacher-created virtual field trips are listed at the end of this chapter.

What Are Some Advantages of Online Virtual Field Trips?

There are several advantages of virtual field trips, whether they are pre-made tours that can be found on the Internet or if they are teacher-created. Some of the advantages are:

- Cost is usually less since no transportation, entrance fees, or meal expenses are involved.
- Permission slips do not need to be sent out or returned.
- Liability problems are eliminated.
- The trip can be scheduled at the convenience of the teacher to match the curriculum.
- The teacher or students can control the speed of the presentation.
- Students or teachers can access the virtual field trip as often as they wish and spend as much or as little time on the site as they want.
- Many students can easily access a site that might not be able to accommodate several students or classes at one time in a traditional visit.
- Virtual field trips are not affected by inclement weather, nor do they require much physical exertion, which might need to be considered if persons with disabilities are included in a class that is taking an actual field trip.

- Virtual field trips often include a variety of formats (audio, video, and text), appealing to many different learning styles.
- Virtual field trips can remove barriers of historical time and geographical location.

The following workshop is intended to introduce teachers to the benefits of conducting virtual field trips.

Planning

Before conducting a workshop dealing with virtual field trips you should become familiar with several of the sites produced online. Actually taking some of the trips will most likely increase your enthusiasm for the topic, and you will be ready to offer some worthwhile suggestions to the teachers participating in the staff development. Although we are using an upper elementary level topic for the workshop demonstration, this presentation can be geared to teachers of any grade level. Therefore, it is important for you to know workshop participants' grade levels and subject areas. This staff development topic is an excellent opportunity for further collaboration with teachers, but you will need to be knowledgeable about their curriculum content and the availability of quality virtual field trip sites in their disciplines.

This workshop provides an excellent opportunity to award door prizes that are related to the topic, such as tickets to museums, historical locations, zoos, or theme parks that could be possible future classroom virtual tours. Other door prize ideas include "trips" to local businesses: a beauty salon, a movie theater, a restaurant, or a supermarket. Often local merchants are willing to donate such "trips."

A bulletin board of pictures from the various sites that are going to be visited during the workshop can pique the interest of possible participants if displayed a few weeks before the workshop. These pictures can be downloaded from the sites. Printing the pictures on photo paper can make a particularly attractive bulletin board.

 Length of Time

This workshop is relatively straightforward and will not involve a great deal of attention to individual participants. Conducting this workshop involves approximately 60 to 90 minutes. Your individual attention in collaborative follow-up activities will involve additional time.

 Materials and Equipment

All participants in this workshop need computers with high-speed Internet access. Some of the virtual field trip sites that the participants will explore have numerous graphics and video clips; therefore you want to reduce the amount of time to download the sites. Also, be sure that the latest versions of Internet browsers and the necessary plug-ins have been installed on the computers.

Getting Participants

Try to emphasize the fun that participants can have by taking part in this workshop. Some teachers have not viewed virtual field trips and many are not aware of the interesting and exciting field trips available online. Teachers may have given up on the idea of actual field trips because of some of the complications involved; thus, it is important to share with them how some of these problems can be eliminated or decreased with virtual field trips. It is probably not necessary to severely limit the number of participants but you will need to request an RSVP in your invitation to make certain that you have enough useable computers. Use the Field Trip Tickets provided on the CD-ROM as reminders to participants who respond to the RSVP. Placing the tickets in respondents' mailboxes a couple of days prior to the workshop will serve as an excellent reminder.

 Deciding on Activities

The purpose of this staff development presentation is to introduce teachers to the use of virtual field trips. Workshop objectives include:

- Define virtual field trips.
- Discuss how virtual field trips can be incorporated into the curriculum.
- Take a virtual field trip.
- Identify criteria of an effective virtual field trip.
- Explore virtual field trips.

 Preparing the Materials

You will need the following items before conducting this workshop:

- Computers with high-speed Internet access
- Agendas
- Handouts of the PowerPoint presentation with three slides per page and lines for taking notes
- Resources handouts
- Evaluation forms
- Door prizes

Conducting the Workshop

Before the participants arrive, prepare folders for each participant and place them next to each computer. Each folder should contain an agenda, the PowerPoint hand-out, the resources handout, and an evaluation form. Printing or copying items on different colored paper will facilitate the workshop process, allowing you to easily refer to color-coded handouts throughout the presentation.

Welcome your participants and begin the PowerPoint presentation immediately. When working in groups allow participants to freely share their enthusiasm about some of the sites and encourage them to do further exploration of sites in their classrooms.

Evaluation

 This workshop, like the others in this book, needs to contain a meaningful evaluation. Include items that deal with the clarity of the presentation, as well as the participants' interest in other workshops that involve making lesson plans for virtual field trips, taking trips that involve more than one online site, or creating virtual field trips.

Follow-Up Activities

Contact the teachers through e-mail and offer your assistance in the implementation of the virtual field trip that they plan to take in their classrooms or in the computer lab. It is important to check the availability of a computer lab for a virtual field trip. If a computer teacher is on the school staff, you will want to collaboratively work with that person, as well as with the teacher.

There are other staff development workshops that can be developed as sequels to this one. You could help teachers write specific lesson plans for the implementation of virtual field trips. Teachers might want to learn how to become involved in online expeditions or conduct virtual field trips that involve several sites—or even create their own online field trips, using digital cameras, videos, and Web-authoring software. Many teachers will be enthusiastic about virtual field trips, so be prepared to continue with additional staff development for some participants.

 Final Tips

☑ Emphasize the importance of finding an outstanding destination that will pique the interest of the students, as well as enhance the curriculum area.

☑ Remind teachers that conducting a virtual field trip involves careful planning, preparation, and follow up to be successful.

☑ Tell the teachers to preview their virtual field trip online before taking the students on the trip to make certain all links are operating and there have been no major changes in the site since initially accessing it.

☑ Encourage student input in all aspects of conducting a virtual field trip.

References

Ashton, T.M. (2002). New virtual field trips. *Roeper Review, 24* (4), 236-237. Retrieved June 23, 2003, from ProQuest database.

Cox-Petersen, Anne M. & Melber, Leah M. (2001). Using technology to prepare and extend field trips. *The Clearing House, 75* (1), 18-20.

Stevenson, Stephanie. (2001). Discover and create your own field trips. *Multimedia Schools, 8* (40), 40-45.

Tuthill, Gail & Klemm, Barbara, (2002). Virtual field trips: Alternatives to actual field trips. *International Journal of Instructional Media, 29* (4), 453-468.

Wilton, Jan & Foley, Kim (2003). A virtual trip into real technology standards. *Multimedia Schools, 10* (1), 38-40.

Selected Resources

Books

Cooper, Gail & Cooper, Gary. (2001). *New virtual field trips*. Englewood, CA: Libraries Unlimited/Teacher Ideas Press.

This book includes an annotated collection of Web sites dealing with virtual field trips. The book is divided into thirteen chapters that cover different content areas. An introductory chapter provides examples on how to incorporate a Web site into the curriculum.

Foley, Kim. (2002). *The big pocket guide to using & creating field trips*. Spokane, WA: Persistent Vision.

This guide provides K-12 educators with information on how to create virtual field trips. The book is intended to help educators learn how to get started in this area, but it does not include extensive listings of virtual field trips on the Web.

Web Sites

Innovative Teaching. (2003). *The best virtual field trips online*. Retrieved August 29, 2003, from <http://surfaquarium.com/virtual.htm>

Guidelines for conducting virtual field trips are included, as well as a long listing of sites that offer virtual field trips. The sites are arranged alphabetically and need to be browsed in order to find curriculum areas and grade levels.

Middle School.Net. (n.d.). *Field trips & exhibits*. Retrieved August 29, 2003, from <http://www.middleschool.net/curlink/virtual.htm>

Virtual field trips that go to one destination are featured on this site, which specializes in middle school education. The sites are arranged alphabetically without any division into content areas so one must browse to find an appropriate topic to match the curriculum.

The Teacher's Guide. (n.d.). *Virtual field trips*. Retrieved August 29, 2003, from <http://www.theteachersguide.com/virtualtours.html>

Virtual field trips on this site are one-destination (although some have additional links) and are divided into the following areas: general, museums, and exhibits. There does not appear to be any particular arrangement of the sites within those divisions.

Tramline. (2003). *Welcome to the virtual field trips at Tramline*. Retrieved August 29, 2003, from <http://www.field-guides.com/vft/index.htm>

This award-winning site provides annotated virtual field trips, using a variety of "threaded" sites for each theme. Content areas include science, social studies, technology, and miscellaneous. A Teacher Resource Tour provides an introduction to virtual field trips, as well as some comparisons of virtual and real field trips.

 Materials Available on the Accompanying CD-ROM

- Flyer
- Field Trip Tickets
- Agenda
- PowerPoint Presentation: Conducting Virtual Field Trips
- Resources Handout
- Evaluation

Chapter 8

Compact It:

Creating Electronic

Portfolios

Background and Information Needs

The emphasis on assessment in classrooms in the 1990s and early 21st century initiated the development of new measures of evaluating students' educational progress in schools throughout the United States. One of the assessment measures that became very popular and continues in some schools today is the use of student portfolios. Portfolios were first developed as collections of print items produced by students; however, emerging technologies have popularized the use of electronic portfolios.

What Is a Portfolio?

A portfolio is "an organized collection of complex, performance-based evidence that indicates one's growth, goals, and current knowledge and skills needed to be competent in a role or area of expertise" (Campbell, Melenyzer, Nettles & Wyman, 2000, p. 151). There are various types of portfolios, usually distinguished by their purpose. Professionals frequently develop and utilize portfolios to gain employment or to provide documentation for promotions, tenure, fund seeking, consultancies and other similar activities.

At the K-12 level of education a portfolio is a purposeful collection of a student's work to demonstrate his or her efforts, growth, and accomplishments. It is sometimes used for assessment, but "across time can also provide an invaluable snapshot of a student's current skills, as well as provide an opportunity for the student to reflect on his or her growth as a learner" (Siegle, 2002). A student portfolio is more than just a group of papers or projects. A portfolio should include learner goals, as well as carefully selected items (artifacts). Written guidelines for the selection of items are needed so the portfolio does not become a haphazard collection. It is usually recommended that students and teachers cooperatively select the portfolio items. Additionally, some teacher feedback and student self-reflection should be included in a student's portfolio. If the portfolio is to be used for assessment, carefully designed rubrics for evaluating the work should be provided to the students. In some schools the teacher may want to base these rubrics on specific standards.

The terms "electronic portfolio" or "computer-based portfolio" are used to describe portfolios that are saved in electronic formats. They contain the same type of information as the traditional print portfolio but the information is collected, stored, and managed electronically.

Why Develop Electronic Portfolios?

There are many reasons to make student portfolios electronic. One of the primary reasons is that storage space is greatly decreased. An electronic portfolio program also makes it possible for easy transfer of information; thus, an individual disk or CD-ROM can be created to transport a student's documents from teacher to teacher or school to school. It relatively easy and inexpensive to create and maintain electronic portfolios using today's technology.

Electronic portfolios also enable students to collect and organize items in a variety of formats and demonstrate a wide dimension of learning. For example, text, graphics, sound, and video can all be combined in an electronic portfolio. Writing samples, solutions to math problems, student art work, a digitized tape of a student's speech, and a digital video of an explanation of a science project are samples of artifacts that can all be combined into one portfolio. Additionally, students increase their technology skills if they can learn to produce and help maintain their own electronic portfolios.

How Are Electronic Portfolios Created?

When developing an electronic portfolio, one must select the storage medium. In most schools four options exist: floppy disks, zip disks, CD-ROMs and the school or district server. Although floppy disks are an easy, inexpensive format, they have storage limitations, making them insufficient to include any audio or video files. Zip disks can generally store 70 to 170 times more information than floppy disks, while CD-ROMs have almost 500 times more storage space than floppy disks. CD-ROMS are also very inexpensive if purchased in bulk (Siegle, 2002). CD-ROMs come in two formats: rewritable and ones that can be recorded only once. Teachers and students can continually add to rewritable disks, but these rewritable disks have the disadvantage of being able to be read only in computers with rewritable drives. School or district servers have the advantage of not involving additional costs; however, access to the server is usually restricted and students and teachers would most likely not be able to directly edit portfolios housed on the server. The final decision on the storage and presentation media must take into account the intended audience, available hardware and software, the technology skills of the persons creating the portfolio, and whether the use of electronic portfolios is building or district-wide.

There are several available software applications that can aid in the production of electronic portfolios. Microsoft products such as Word, PowerPoint, Publisher, and FrontPage work well. Netscape's Composer, Macromedia's Dreamweaver, and Knowledge Adventure's HyperStudio can also meet the needs of a wide variety of portfolio designs (Heath, 2003). Some software programs such as Grady Portfolio and Chalk & Wire's ePortfolio are designed specifically for creating electronic portfolios.

Since the primary focus of creating an electronic portfolio should be on content, rather than on technology skills, it is highly recommended that teachers and students become familiar with the software before trying to develop a portfolio. Thus, the creator of the portfolio will not be overwhelmed with the mastery of technology skills. Once a basic portfolio is produced additional technology skills can be learned to provide more sophistication or flexibility to the portfolio.

After the storage format and software applications are selected, the development of an electronic portfolio is very similar to that of a paper portfolio. Initially, teachers should establish learner goals and communicate these to the students. The next step is for students to collect artifacts or items that relate to those goals. The collection can include everything that might be considered as a final portfolio artifact. Keeping some of the items in a manila folder can cut down on the time to scan them. Also, putting items in an electronic format before selections of portfolio items are made can facilitate the process. The next step is choosing the final artifacts, based on the teacher's written criteria. This process is particularly important as only items that serve a particular purpose or objective should be included. After selections are made, a fourth step is reflection. In this step, students should be led to reflect on what they have learned from producing a particular item. These reflections can be included in the portfolio in a written format or in another format such as audio recordings. With younger students, teacher feedback and comments might also be included in this step. A final step involves projection—what needs to be done in the future. This can include how to improve skills, what a student still wants or needs to learn, and how to continue to grow (Heath, 2003). Such projection will help students develop future goals and objectives.

The entire portfolio can be "graded" if the portfolio is being used for assessment purposes, or it can be used for showcasing student work. Rubrics are often used to grade or score a portfolio. These rubrics contain categories dealing with the content of the items, the writing mechanics (spelling, grammar, punctuation), the student reflections on the selected artifacts, and the overall design of the portfolio.

Planning

One of the first steps that you will need to do to plan this workshop is to decide on the software you want to use to develop a portfolio. If you have access to more than one type, try some out to see the advantages and disadvantages of each one. You will also want to consider the technology skills of your participants when you make your final software decision. If you decide to use a software program that is unfamiliar to the participants, you should hold a pre-workshop session that explains how to use the software. Be sure to give participants time to practice so they will be comfortable with the program when it is used in the portfolio workshop. This pre-workshop session will help teachers be able to focus on the content of your electronic portfolio presentation, rather than become frustrated with the technology. To prepare for your workshop, it is important that you develop a portfolio using the workshop software and presentation media. By doing so you will be able to practice the steps involved in the workshop and you will also have an item that you can use for possible demonstration.

If you plan to use the school or district server for the presentation of portfolios, you should meet with the person who maintains the server. Ask this person how to use the server for this purpose and consider inviting him or her to your workshop to assist in the presentation.

For this workshop we have assumed that the teacher participants have knowledge of and practice with Microsoft's PowerPoint and Word applications, as well as with scanners and digital cameras. If teachers are not proficient in these areas, you need to offer a pre-workshop session or one-on-one assistance.

Since this workshop is technologically intensive, it is important for you to practice the presentation, particularly the section dealing with the processes in the template. If you do not use a scanner and a digital camera on a regular basis, you should practice these skills as well since the participants will need your assistance.

When you announce the workshop, provide teachers with a few weeks' notice, and ask them to bring one or two print copies of a student's classroom work. Participants should also bring along a brief biography of the student, including the student's special interests. The student can be asked to write the biography. If participants are able to take a digital photo of a project (model, artwork, etc.) produced by the same student, ask that they bring a disk with this image, as well as a photo of the student. All of these items will be used in the workshop.

 Length of Time

The length of time for this workshop will depend on the number of participants. Each participant will be inserting items into a template to create an electronic portfolio. They will also be scanning print copies of student projects and will be working with digital photos. If there is only one scanner available for use, the required time for the workshop will be increased. Most likely some of the teachers will need individual assistance when actually putting items into the student portfolio. If ten or fewer teachers are involved, this workshop should take 60 to 90 minutes.

 Materials and Equipment

Each participant will need an individual computer with Microsoft's PowerPoint installed. Additionally, you will need a similar computer for your workshop presentation.

Prior to the date of the workshop, remind participants to bring a digital photo (on disk) or a regular photo of one student, a short biography of that student (which can be written by the student or teacher), and print or digital copies of the student's classroom work.

Getting Participants

This workshop should not be mandatory, unless the school or district requires the use of electronic portfolios. The encouragement and support of administrators will be helpful in increasing attendance. However, because this workshop will be technologically intensive you should limit the number of participants to no more than ten. Send out invitations or flyers for this workshop a few weeks ahead of time so teachers have time to select the items that you are requesting them to bring. The flyer should include a message of reassurance and an offer of help for teachers who might feel anxious about the technology involved in the workshop. Also, because you will need a computer for each participant, be sure to request an RSVP.

 Deciding on Activities

Do not be too ambitious when deciding on the goals and objectives for this workshop. If you are successful in having each of the participants understand the benefits of electronic portfolios and have them begin to make a portfolio for one student in their classroom, they will be able to build on their knowledge and skills. Some possible objectives for the staff development session include:

- Verbalize the definition and uses of a portfolio.
- Identify the advantages of an electronic portfolio.
- Discuss how to create an electronic portfolio.
- View completed electronic portfolios.
- Develop an electronic portfolio using a sample template.

 Preparing the Materials

You will need the following items for this staff development workshop:

- An agenda
- A CD-ROM or 3.5 inch floppy disk, with a prepared e-portfolio template for each participant
- Scanner(s)
- Digital camera(s)
- Computers with Microsoft Word and PowerPoint programs installed
- A handout of the PowerPoint presentation, with three slides per page and lines for taking notes
- A handout of selected resources
- An evaluation form

For each participant place the following items into one side of a double-pocketed folder: the agenda, PowerPoint handout, CD-ROM or 3.5 inch floppy disk, selected resources handout, and an evaluation form.

If you are serving refreshments, they will also need to be prepared ahead of time and placed in a location away from the computers or other electronic equipment.

Conducting the Workshop

As the participants arrive at the workshop hand each of them an agenda. The first item on the agenda should be a time to scan items or use a digital camera. If teachers forget to bring the requested student materials, have them retrieve them from their classrooms. During this time you should have refreshments available. Ideally, these beginning activities should not take more than 20 minutes. When all participants are finished scanning or taking pictures, instruct them to take a seat at one of the computers, where you have placed folders containing the workshop items. Tell the participants to remove the PowerPoint handout so they can take notes during the presentation. When you come to the PowerPoint slide that has links to student portfolio samples, you may want to select different links (perhaps from local schools) or add additional links. We have included samples of both secondary school and elementary school electronic portfolios. However, you should choose specific portfolio sites according to grade levels or perhaps subject areas, depending on the make-up of your audience.

When the teachers begin to create their own student portfolios, they may need some individual assistance. If there are others who can help with this portion of the workshop, it will facilitate this process. Circulate through the room while the teachers work on their student portfolios and remember to encourage them in their efforts. It is not essential that the teachers enter all the items into the electronic portfolios, but be sure that they understand the processes involved so they can complete the portfolios on their own.

Evaluation

For this workshop, the evaluation should question whether the information in the staff development presentation was presented effectively and whether the participants gained the understanding and skills to create electronic portfolios. You also should ask if any teachers would like to participate in an additional workshop that would help them include audio and video items in their student portfolios.

Follow-Up Activities

A day or two after the staff development presentation, send an e-mail to the teachers thanking them for their participation and offering your continued assistance with the creation of their student portfolios. When you see the teachers during the next few weeks, inquire about their progress with their portfolio projects. When some of the teachers have completed one of more student portfolios for their classes, ask if you can showcase the portfolios at a faculty meeting. Be sure to get parental permission whenever student portfolios are shown in a faculty meeting or in any public setting. If a school technology staff person or anyone else assists you with the workshop, follow up with a thank you note and perhaps a small gift of appreciation.

Final Tips

☑ Encourage teachers to teach their students how to create and maintain their own electronic portfolios. This will substantially cut down on the amount of time needed by the teachers for this process and will provide the students with opportunities to gain useful technology skills.

☑ If you are showcasing the work of students on publicly accessible sites, be sure to get the written permission of parents to include photos or any information that would identify students. Using only first names of students and not including complete biographical information is sometimes the best option in these cases.

☑ If the teachers in your school want to develop sophisticated electronic portfolios, consider investing in a software program that is designed specifically for the purpose of creating computer-based portfolios. Some of the programs are relatively expensive, but they make portfolio development and maintenance easier.

☑ Offer to assist teachers who want to make professional portfolios, such as those teachers applying for National Board Certification.

References

Campbell, Dorothy M., Melenyzer, Beverly J., Nettles, Diane H. & Wyman, Richard, Jr. (2000). *Portfolio and performance assessment in teacher education*. Boston: Allyn & Bacon.

Heath, Marilyn. (2003). Electronic portfolios for authentic professional development. *Library Media Connection, 21* (6), 38-40.

Siegle, Del. (2002). Technology: Creating a living portfolio: Documenting student growth with electronic portfolios. *Gifted Child Today, 25* (3), 60-63.

Selected Resources

Books

Ash, Linda E. (2000). *Electronic student portfolios*. Glenview, IL: Pearson Professional Development.

The author shows educators how to use technology, including audio, video, text, and still images to make student portfolios for assessment purposes. She also includes information about how to get students to assume responsibility for collecting, selecting, and reflecting on the work that is placed in their portfolios.

Cole, Donna J., Ryan, Charles W., Kick, Frank, & Mathies, Donna. (1999). *Portfolios across the curriculum* (2nd ed.). Thousand Oaks, CA: Corwin Press.

This easy-to-read guide to the use of portfolios is written for K-12 teachers. It explains the purposes for initiating the portfolio process in schools. The use of multi-media technology in developing portfolios is included.

Web Sites

Barrett, Helen. (2003). *Information about electronic portfolio development.* Retrieved September 24, 2003, from <http://electronicportfolios.com/portfolios/bibliography.html>

You won't want to miss this site. It contains a wealth of information about electronic portfolios, including many articles the author has written on the topic. The bibliography link contains a long list of resources.

Curry, Rob (2003). *Student e-portfolios.* Retrieved October 6, 2003, from <http://www.everyschool.org/u/vinci/eportfolio/eportemplate.html>

This page contains links to the e-portfolios of students in Mr. Rob Curry's fifth grade class at Vinci Park School in San Jose, California. The students created their portfolios with the help of a template that also appears on the site, with specific directions to the students. A variety of projects in different areas of the curriculum are included.

Lankes, Anna Maria D. (1995). *Electronic portfolios: A new idea in assessment.* Retrieved September, 26, 2003, from <http://ericit.org/digests/EDO-IR-1995-09.shtml>

This site provides a quick, but excellent, introduction to the definition of portfolios, their uses, and the creation of electronic portfolios.

MEHS student portfolios (2003). Retrieved October 6, 2003, from <http://www.mehs.edu.state.ak.us/portfolios/portfolio.html>

This outstanding site provided by Mt. Edgecumbe High School in Sitka, Alaska includes several samples of electronic portfolios created by high school students during the past few years. Many of the portfolios contain multimedia projects that require a fair amount of time to download but they are well worth the wait. The site also contains a link to some portfolio help pages for creating electronic portfolios.

Worcester, Tammy. (1997). *Electronic portfolios.* Retrieved September 24, 2003, from <http://www.essdack.org/port/index.html>

This well-designed Web site provides information on why to use student portfolios, how to create them and what to include. Two examples of student portfolios are provided, as well as a rubric for assessing a portfolio. Pages of the Web site can be printed and reproduced for classroom use.

 Materials Available on the Accompanying CD-ROM

- Flyer
- Agenda
- PowerPoint Presentation
- Project Template
  This will need to be downloaded onto each CD-ROM used by the participants. The participants will fill in the template with their specific information.
- Evaluation

Notes

Notes

Notes

Notes

Notes

Notes